HADEDA LA LAND

By Stephen Francis & Rico

JACANA

To our loving wives ... who often give us the headlines, the deadlines ... and sometimes even the punchlines

Published in 2017 in South Africa by
Jacana Media
10 Orange Street, Auckland Park, 2092
PO Box 291784, Melville, 2109
www.jacana.co.za

ISBN 978-1-4314-2567-9
Job number 003106
Printed and bound by ABC Press, Cape Town

OTHER MADAM & EVE BOOKS

Madam & Eve Collection (Rapid Phase, 1993, reprint 1999)
Free At Last (Penguin Books, 1994)
All Aboard for the Gravy Train (Penguin Books, 1995)
Somewhere over the Rainbow Nation (Penguin Books, 1996)
Madam & Eve's Greatest Hits (Penguin Books, 1997)
Madams are from Mars, Maids are from Venus (Penguin Books, 1997)
It's a Jungle Out There (David Philip, 1998)
International Maid of Mystery (David Philip, 1999)
Has anyone seen my Vibrating Cellphone? (interactive.Africa, 2000)
The Madams are Restless (Rapid Phase, 2000)
Crouching Madam, Hidden Maid (Rapid Phase, 2001)
Madam & Eve, 10 Wonderful Years (Rapid Phase, 2002)
The Maidtrix (Rapid Phase, 2003)
Gin & Tonic for the Soul (Rapid Phase, 2004)
Desperate Housemaids (Rapid Phase, 2005)
Madams of the Caribbean (Rapid Phase, 2006)
Bring me my (new) Washing Machine (Rapid Phase, 2007)
Madam & Eve Unplugged (Rapid Phase, 2008)
Strike While The Iron Is Hot (Jacana, 2009)

Twilight of the Vuvuzelas (Jacana, 2010)
Mother Anderson's Secret Book of Wit & Wisdom (Jacana, 2011)
The Pothole at the End of the Rainbow (Jacana, 2011)
Twenty (Jacana, 2012)
Keep Calm and Take Another Tea Break (Jacana, 2013)
Send in the Clowns (Jacana, 2014)
Shed Happens (Jacana, 2015)
Take Me to Your Leader (Jacana, 2016)
Jamen sort kaffe er pa mode nu, Madam! (Gyldendal, Denmark, 1995)
Jeg gyver Mandela Skylden for det her! (Gyldendal, Denmark, 1995)
Alt under kontrol I Sydafrika! (Bogfabrikken, Denmark, 1997)
Men alla dricker kaffet svart nufortiden, Madam! (Bokfabrikken, Sweden, 1998)
Madame & Eve, Enfin Libres! (Vents D'Ouest, France, 1997)
Votez Madame & Eve (Vents D'Ouest, France, 1997)
La coupe est pleine (Vents D'Ouest, France, 1998)
Rennue-Ménage à deux (Vents D'Ouest, France, 1999)
En voient de toutes les couleurs (Vents D'Ouest, France, 2000)
Madame vient de Mars, Eve de Venus (Vents D'Ouest, France, 2000)
Madam & Eve (LIKE, Finland, 2005)

MADAM & EVE APPEARS REGULARLY IN:
Mail & Guardian, The Star, Saturday Star, Herald, Mercury, Witness, Daily Dispatch, Cape Times, Pretoria News, Diamond Fields Advertiser, Die Volksblad, EC Today, Kokstad Advertiser, The Namibian.

TO CONTACT MADAM & EVE:
PO Box 413667, Craighall 2024, Johannesburg, South Africa
ricos@rico.co.za
www.madamandeve.co.za

LA LA LAND

HADEDA LA LAND

FIKILE MBALULA LA LAND

BERNING -- YOU'RE **FIRED!**

NO, I'M **NOT!**

YES, YOU ARE! HAND IN YOUR CAR AND CELLPHONE!

WHAT CELLPHONE?!

HAWKS

≷AHEM≷... DID YOU LEAVE THE **KITCHEN** DOOR OPEN?

UH. I MIGHT HAVE. ...WHY?

OH.

DON'T ALL THE HADEDAS IN THE LOUNGE BOTHER GOGO?

NOT REALLY... AS LONG AS THEY DON'T CROSS THE LINE.

WHAT'S "CROSSING THE LINE?"

SLURP.

OH.

FLAP! FLAP! FLAP!!

3

HADEDA DAH!

WHO CHANGED MY RINGTONE TO @#*&$ "HADEDA?!"

NOW WE RUN? NOW WE RUN.

BRRR...

TIC TIC TIC TIC

HADEDALAI LAMA

"GENERAL KNOWLEDGE HOMEWORK QUIZ..."

"QUESTION #1: GIVE AN EXAMPLE OF A SUCCESSFUL COALITION."

"GIN & TONIC."

MADAM & Eve

BY STEPHEN FRANCIS & RICO

OKAY. HOP ON ONE FOOT.

HOP! HOP! HOP! HOP!

GOOD. NOW QUACK LIKE A DUCK.

QUACK! QUACK! QUACK! QUACK!

NICE. NOW BALANCE THIS CHICKEN ON YOUR HEAD.

Cluck?

NOT BAD. NOW JUGGLE THESE FLAMING TORCHES.

Cluck! Cluck! Cluck! Cluck!

OW! OW! OW!

SIZZLE! SIZZLE!

NOW REPEAT AFTER ME: "ZUMA IS A @#*@# IDIOT."

UH... ZUMA IS A @#*@# IDIOT.

©RAPID PHASE-2016

OKAY. THAT'S ENOUGH. WE'LL GET BACK TO YOU.

THANK YOU.

HOW ARE THE "COALITION" NEGOTIATIONS GOING?

LOTS OF FUN!

WAIT UNTIL THEY FIND OUT WE'RE **NOT** ENTERING INTO A COALITION WITH **ANYONE!**

HEE-HEE! **NEXT!**

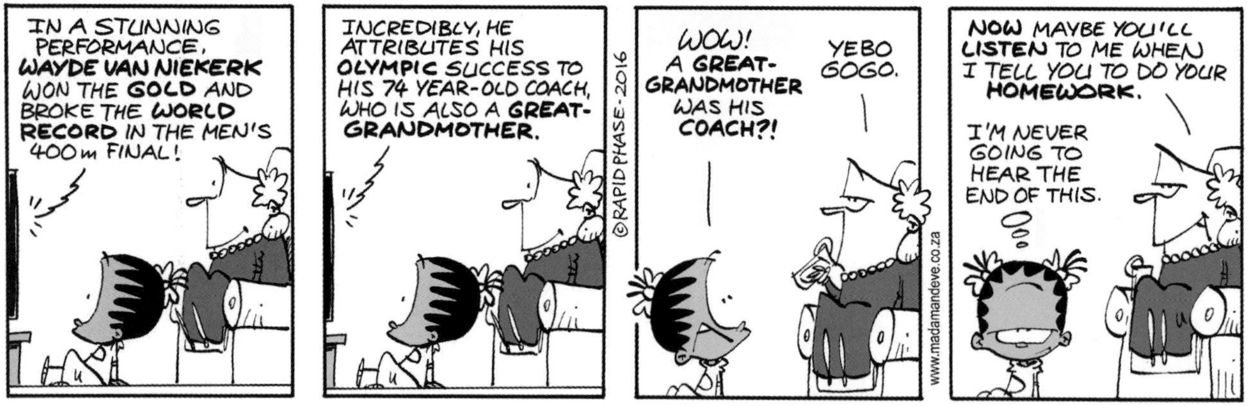
IN A STUNNING PERFORMANCE, WAYDE VAN NIEKERK WON THE GOLD AND BROKE THE WORLD RECORD IN THE MEN'S 400m FINAL!
INCREDIBLY, HE ATTRIBUTES HIS OLYMPIC SUCCESS TO HIS 74 YEAR-OLD COACH, WHO IS ALSO A GREAT-GRANDMOTHER.
©RAPID PHASE·2016
WOW! A GREAT-GRANDMOTHER WAS HIS COACH?!
YEBO GOGO.
www.madamandeve.co.za
NOW MAYBE YOU'LL LISTEN TO ME WHEN I TELL YOU TO DO YOUR HOMEWORK.
I'M NEVER GOING TO HEAR THE END OF THIS.

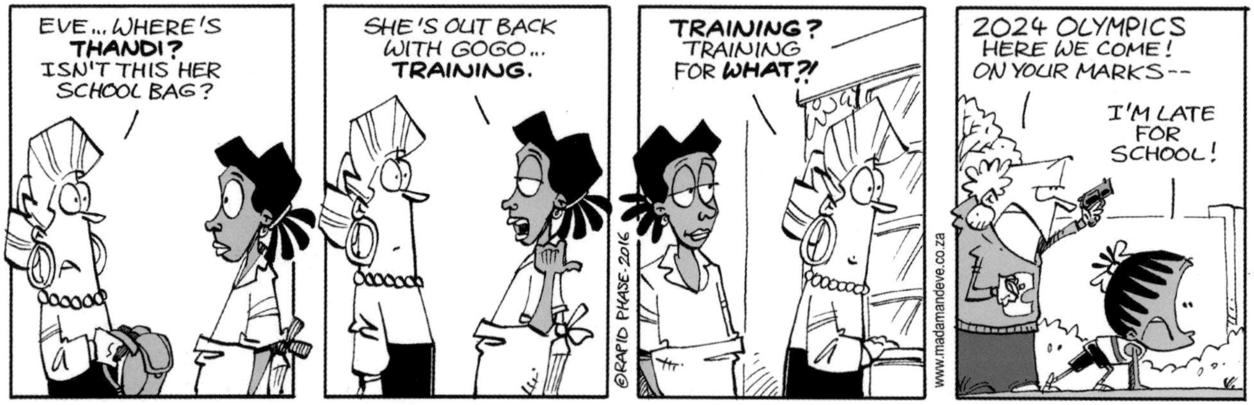
EVE... WHERE'S THANDI? ISN'T THIS HER SCHOOL BAG?
SHE'S OUT BACK WITH GOGO... TRAINING.
©RAPID PHASE·2016
TRAINING? TRAINING FOR WHAT?!
www.madamandeve.co.za
2024 OLYMPICS HERE WE COME! ON YOUR MARKS--
I'M LATE FOR SCHOOL!

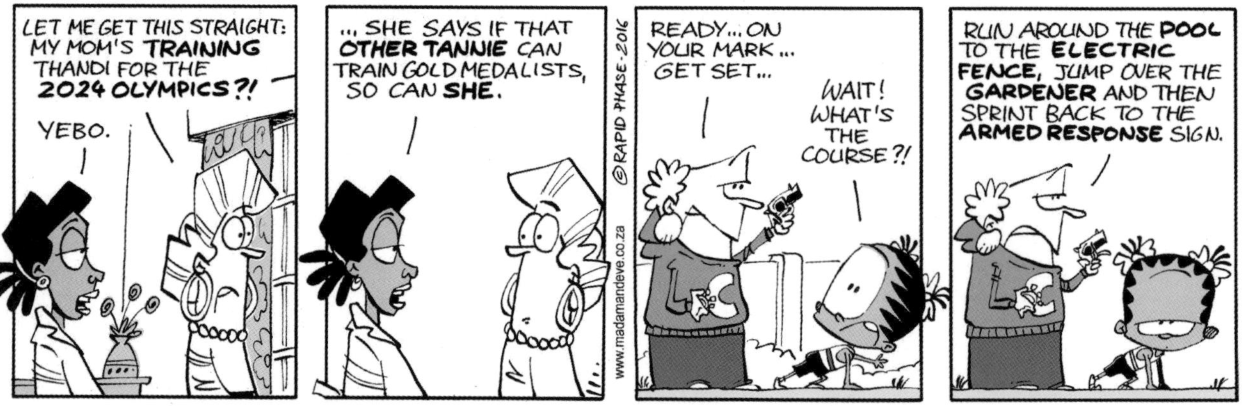
LET ME GET THIS STRAIGHT: MY MOM'S TRAINING THANDI FOR THE 2024 OLYMPICS?!
YEBO.
... SHE SAYS IF THAT OTHER TANNIE CAN TRAIN GOLD MEDALISTS, SO CAN SHE.
©RAPID PHASE·2016
www.madamandeve.co.za
READY... ON YOUR MARK... GET SET...
WAIT! WHAT'S THE COURSE?!
RUN AROUND THE POOL TO THE ELECTRIC FENCE, JUMP OVER THE GARDENER AND THEN SPRINT BACK TO THE ARMED RESPONSE SIGN.

THANDI! WHY DON'T YOU **HAVE** YOUR **HOMEWORK?!**

IT'S NOT MY **FAULT!**

MY **GOGO TRAINER** MADE ME **PRACTICE** ALL WEEK FOR THE **2024 OLYMPICS!**

YOU SHOULD HAVE JUST GONE WITH "MY DOG ATE IT."

I WAS **TELLING** THE **TRUTH!!**

PRINC

I READ A **THEORY** ON THE INTERNET... THAT PRESIDENT **ZUMA** IS ACTUALLY AN **ALIEN.**

HIS MISSION? TO **DESTABILISE** CIVILISATION AND **PAVE** THE WAY FOR A **FULL-SCALE INVASION.**

IMPOSSIBLE.

YOU DON'T THINK HE COULD BE AN **ALIEN?**

NO, **THAT'S** POSSIBLE.

...IT'S THE "**PAVING THE WAY**" PART. FAR TOO MANY **POTHOLES.**

THANDI! WHERE'S YOUR **HOMEWORK?!**

HOW COULD I **POSSIBLY** HAVE **TIME** TO **DO** IT?!

...THE **HAWKS** HAVE DEMANDED I **PRESENT** MYSELF! I'M ALREADY **LATE!**

FINE! DON'T BLAME ME WHEN THE **RAND PLUMMETS!**

PRINCIPAL

Panel 1: THERE'S A **CALL** FOR YOU, MISTER PRESIDENT. — I DON'T WANT TO **TALK** TO ANYONE! **WHO** IS IT?

Panel 2: HE **SAYS** HE'S THE **SON** OF **GOD**.

Panel 3: ⸘GASP!⸘ I **KNEW** IT! I **KNEW** HE'D **RETURN** WHEN THE **ANC** LOST! I'M NOT **HERE!**

Panel 4: ...CAN HE CALL YOU BACK, **MISTER TRUMP?** HE'S **OUT** AT THE MOMENT.

Panel 5: WHO'S **DONALD TRUMP?** — HE'S A **POLITICIAN.**

Panel 6: ...HE LOVES **MONEY,** HE LOVES **POWER,** HE SAYS LOTS OF **SILLY** THINGS THAT DON'T MAKE **SENSE**...

Panel 7: ...AND **MANY** PEOPLE THINK HE SHOULD **NEVER** BE PRESIDENT.

Panel 8: SOUNDS A LOT LIKE **JACOB ZUMA.**

Panel 9: WHAT ARE YOU DOING? — I'M MAKING A LIST OF **SIMILARITIES** BETWEEN **JACOB ZUMA** AND **DONALD TRUMP.**

Panel 10: ...BOTH LOVE **MONEY** AND **LUXURY** HOMES... BOTH HAVE MORE THAN ONE **WIFE**... AND BOTH HIRE **FAMILY** MEMBERS FOR KEY **POSITIONS**...

Panel 11: BOTH HAVE **BIG HEADS** AND OFTEN **SAY** THINGS THAT MAKE **NO** SENSE... AND... UH...

Panel 12: ONE SAYS "YOU'RE **FIRED!**" ...THE OTHER HAS A **FIRE** POOL. — **MOM!!**

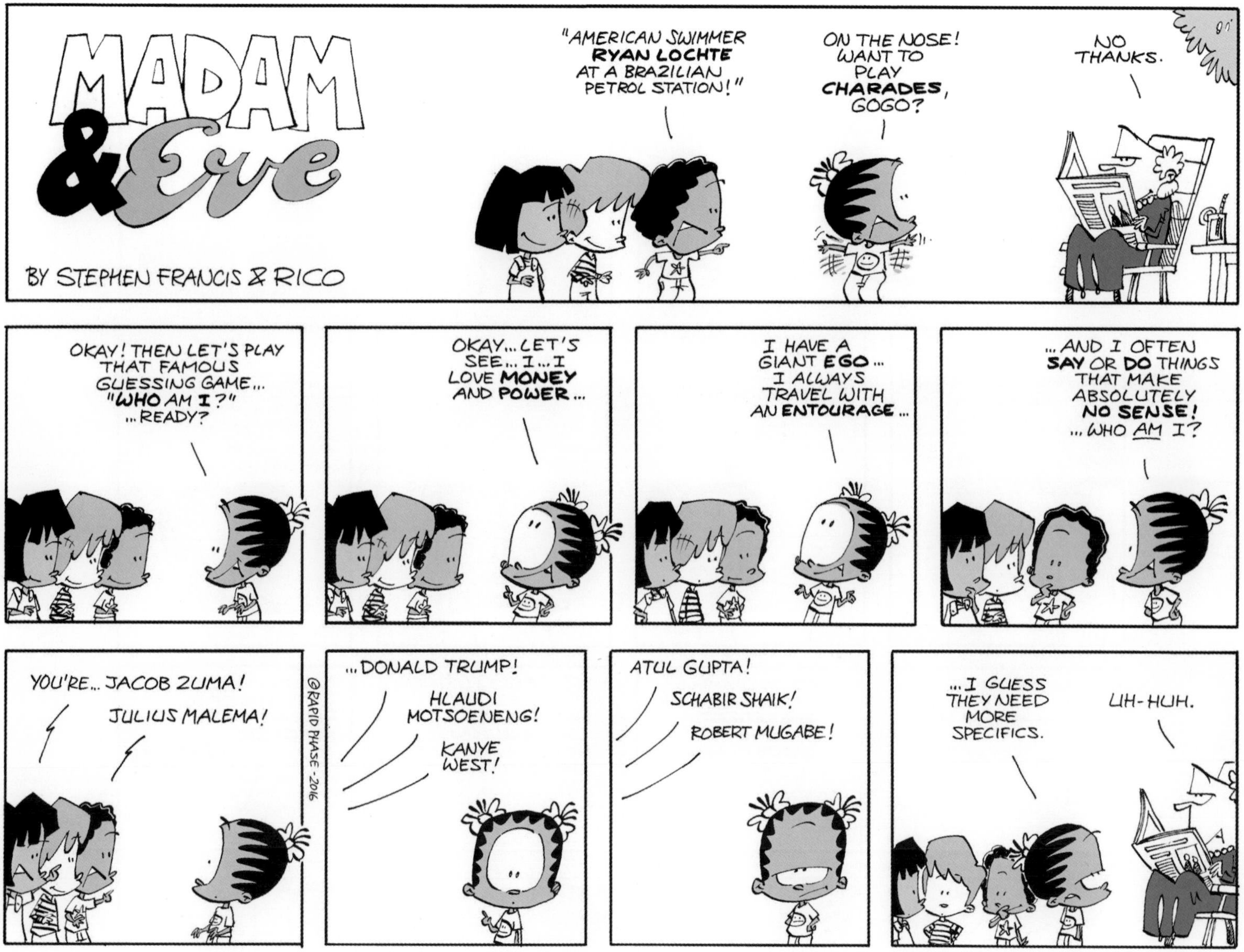
MADAM & Eve
BY STEPHEN FRANCIS & RICO
"AMERICAN SWIMMER RYAN LOCHTE AT A BRAZILIAN PETROL STATION!"
ON THE NOSE! WANT TO PLAY CHARADES, GOGO?
NO THANKS.
OKAY! THEN LET'S PLAY THAT FAMOUS GUESSING GAME... "WHO AM I?" ...READY?
OKAY... LET'S SEE... I... I LOVE MONEY AND POWER...
I HAVE A GIANT EGO... I ALWAYS TRAVEL WITH AN ENTOURAGE...
...AND I OFTEN SAY OR DO THINGS THAT MAKE ABSOLUTELY NO SENSE! ...WHO AM I?
YOU'RE... JACOB ZUMA!
JULIUS MALEMA!
©RAPID PHASE - 2016
...DONALD TRUMP!
HLAUDI MOTSOENENG!
KANYE WEST!
ATUL GUPTA!
SCHABIR SHAIK!
ROBERT MUGABE!
...I GUESS THEY NEED MORE SPECIFICS.
UH-HUH.

REPEAT AFTER ME...

WE TAKE COLLECTIVE RESPONSIBILITY FOR THE ELECTION RESULTS...

IT'S NOT PRESIDENT ZUMA'S FAULT...

RIGHT, CLASS. ENGLISH GRAMMAR QUIZ. YOU HAVE 30 MINUTES! GO!

"QUESTION ONE: GIVE AN EXAMPLE OF A **DANGEROUS PRECEDENT**."

"JACOB ZUMA."

I CAN'T **BELIEVE** I ONLY GOT A "**C**" ON MY ENGLISH QUIZ!

LET ME SEE THAT.

"GIVE AN EXAMPLE OF A **DANGEROUS PRECEDENT**. ...ANSWER: JACOB ZUMA."

YOU'RE CONFUSING "**PRECEDENT**" WITH "**PRESIDENT**." JACOB ZUMA IS **NOT** A DANGEROUS PRESIDENT.

ALTHOUGH... COME TO **THINK** OF IT... I'M CALLING YOUR **TEACHER**.

MOM!

THE HAWK | DOCTOR SPIN

WANTED
PRAVIN GORDHAN

REDSHOT

NATIONALISE MINES!
NATIONALISE BANKS!

FIREPOOL

NUCLEAR DEAL...
JUNK STATUS...
HEH. HEH. HEH.

ECONOMIC SUICIDE SQUAD

Coming soon to a theatre near you.

WHAT'S **WRONG**, COUNCILMAN VUSI?

WHAT'S "**WRONG**?!" HAVE YOU SEEN THE **COST-CUTTING** MEMO FROM THE NEW **MAYOR**?!

NO MORE **PARTIES**! NO MORE **DINNERS**! NO MORE OVERSEAS **TRIPS** ON TAXPAYER'S **MONEY**!!

I MEAN, I'M A **PUBLIC SERVANT**! ...WHAT'S **LEFT**?!

UH... ACTUALLY **SERVING** THE PUBLIC?

PLEASE. ...GET **REAL** MY LIFE IS **OVER**!

NO WORK NO FOOD

OKAY. I'M FEELING GENEROUS. HERE'S **TEN** BUCKS.

COULD YOU MAKE IT **TWENTY**?

NO WOR NO FOO

TWENTY?! WHY SHOULD I **DOUBLE** IT?!

NO WOR NO FOO

WE'VE FORMED A **COALITION**.

NO WORK NO FOOD | NO JOB NO MONEY

AND IN OTHER NEWS: ECONOMISTS SAY **PRESIDENT ZUMA** AND HIS SUPPORTERS WILL LIKELY INITIATE A "**CONTAINMENT** STRATEGY" ...TO **CONTAIN** AND **DISEMPOWER** FINANCE MINISTER **PRAVIN GORDHAN.**

MISTER GORDHAN-- YOU'RE DUE FOR YOUR NEXT APPOINTMENT!

COMING.

JIGGLE! JIGGLE!

HEY!! THE **DOOR** WON'T--

JIGGLE! JIGGLE!

SLAM!!

OPEN UP! DAMMIT!

HEH. HEH. HEH.

DEMONSTRATION MISCOMMUNICATION

IT'S **OCCUPY** LUTHULI HOUSE! **OCCUPY!!**

OCCUPY LUTHULI HOUSE

ZUMA MUST RESIGN

Question #3:
Jacob Zuma is what we call a **"sitting president."** True or false?

(And **explain** your answer.)

"TRUE! ...HE **SITS** IN LIMOS, HE **SITS** IN AEROPLANES, HE **SITS** IN HIS FIREPOOL."

MADAM & Eve

BY STEPHEN FRANCIS & RICO

Mother Goose Rhymes for South Africa

I'M A LITTLE **DESPOT** SHORT AND STOUT PEOPLE CAN SEE THROUGH ME... I'LL SOON BE **OUT**.

HEH.HEH.HEH.HEH.HE

TINKER, TAILOR, SOLDIER, SPY. PICK A JOB AND I'LL BE ONE. **REDEPLOYMENT'S** SO MUCH FUN.

IT'S RAINING, IT'S POURING. THE OLD MAN IS SNORING. **CLIMATE CHANGE**, PLEASE GO AWAY. COME AGAIN SOME OTHER DAY.

HLAUDI BE NIMBLE, HLAUDI BE QUICK, PLEASE SOMEONE, GIVE HLAUDI A GOOD, SWIFT **KICK!**

KICK!

THREE **SCARED MICE!** SEE HOW THEY RUN! SEE HOW THEY RUN! THEY ALL RAN TO THE HIGH COURT, TO FIGHT THE CAPTURE OF STATE REPORT... THREE SCARED MICE!

© RAPID PHASE – 2016

JACK SPRAT COULD EAT NO FAT, HIS WIFE COULD EAT NO LEAN. THEY COULDN'T **AFFORD** THEIR FOOD THESE DAYS, THE RAND'S NOT WORTH A BEAN.

THIS IS THE **HOUSE** THAT **ZUMA** BUILT. THIS IS THE **TAXPAYER** THAT GAVE UP THE TAX THAT PAID FOR THE HOUSE THAT ZUMA BUILT.

JACK AND JILL WENT UP THE HILL TO JOIN A "FEES MUST FALLER". JACK WAS BEATEN DOWN AND BROKE HIS CROWN, AND JILL WAS ARRESTED LATER.

DON'T TELL ANYONE... BUT WE'VE FORMED OUR OWN **SECRET ROGUE UNIT**.

I SEE. ..."WHAT EXACTLY IS A "SECRET ROGUE UNIT?"

HARD TO SAY...

..., SOME PEOPLE SAY THEY REALLY **EXIST**. ...OTHERS SAY THEY'RE **MADE UP** FOR **POLITICAL GAIN**.

HEY! WANNA SEE THE COOL "**SECRET ROGUE UNIT**" LOGO WE DESIGNED?

...GO PLAY OUTSIDE.

THIS JUST IN ... PRESIDENT **ZUMA** HAS **PAID BACK** THE R 7.8 MILLION OWED FOR THE UPGRADES ON HIS **NKANDLA** HOME.

HELLO, HOW CAN I **HELP** YOU TODAY?

I'D LIKE TO **BORROW** R 7.8 MILLION LIKE **PRESIDENT ZUMA**.

SECURITY.

LET'S SEE... I HAVE A BIG HOUSE A CAR... SOME LAND...

SECURITY!!

I JUST **TOLD** YOU! I HAVE A **HOUSE**, A **CAR** --

VBS BANK

I THINK HE MEANT THE **OTHER** KIND OF SECURITY.

THANKS.

MADAM & Eve

BY STEPHEN FRANCIS & RICO

©RAPID PHASE · 2016

WHAT AM I MISSING HERE?

CAN YOU KEEP A SECRET?

WE'VE FORMED OUR OWN TOP SECRET **ROGUE UNIT.**

I **SEE.** AND WHAT EXACTLY DOES A "TOP SECRET ROGUE UNIT" **DO?**

IT DEPENDS ON WHO YOU **ASK.**

THE **FINANCE MINISTER** SAYS IT DOESN'T **EXIST**, BUT THE **ANC** SAYS IT'S SUPER POWERFUL.

SO BASICALLY, WE'RE **STRADDLING** THE **FENCE** ... WAITING TO SEE WHAT **DIRECTION** WE SHOULD **TAKE.**

HOWEVER, WE **COULD** LET YOU IN ON THE **GROUND FLOOR** FOR A TEN BUCK **JOINING FEE.**

SLAM!!

... MAYBE IF WE SHOWED HER OUR SECRET ROGUE HANDSHAKE.

AFTER HER GIN & TONIC ... SHE'LL BE MUCH MORE AGREEABLE.

SO WHAT **IS** "CORRUPTION" ANYWAY,... AND HOW DOES IT **WORK**?

OKAY, SUPPOSE...

..., I TOLD YOUR **TEACHER** I'D GIVE HER **100 BUCKS** TO GIVE YOU AN "A" IN ENGLISH. WHAT WOULD YOU SAY?

I'D SAY... SHE PROBABLY WOULD HAVE TAKEN **75**... AND YOU COULD HAVED SAVED YOURSELF **25 BUCKS.**

THIS IS GOING TO TAKE **LONGER** THAN I THOUGHT.

WAIT A SECOND... I STILL DON'T **UNDERSTAND** THIS WHOLE **CORRUPTION** THING.

OK...

LET'S SAY,...YOU'RE A **TRAFFIC COP** AND I RAN A RED ROBOT. WOULD YOU GIVE ME A **TICKET**?

YES.

..., SUPPOSE I OFFERED TO BUY YOU A **COOLDRINK** INSTEAD. WOULD YOU **TAKE** IT?

DEPENDS...

...HOW **THIRSTY** AM I?

THIS IS **DEFINITELY** GOING TO TAKE LONGER THAN I THOUGHT.

I THINK I **UNDERSTAND** NOW. WHAT DO YOU CALL A POLITICIAN WHO GETS **RICH** IN OFFICE?

ALLEGEDLY CORRUPT.

WHAT DO YOU CALL A POLITICIAN WHOSE **FRIENDS** GET **RICH** WHILE IN OFFICE?

ALLEGEDLY CORRUPT.

WHAT DO YOU CALL A POLITICIAN WHO GETS **RICH**, WHOSE **FRIENDS** GET **RICH**, WHOSE **FAMILY** GETS **RICH** AND HE DOES **WHATEVER** HE WANTS?

...MISTER PRESIDENT.

MOM!!

The world can be a cruel place.

But YOU can make a difference.

So pick up the phone and give generously.

HELP STOP PRESIDENT ABUSE

"EACH TIME I COME HERE... I AM ABUSED BY MEMBERS OF PARLIAMENT..."

MADAM & Eve

BY STEPHEN FRANCIS & RICO

AND IN OTHER NEWS, PRESIDENT **ZUMA** HAS SAID THAT THE ANC IS **STILL LEADING** THE COUNTRY...

...ALTHOUGH WE MIGHT NOT BE **AWARE** OF IT.

PRESIDENT ZUMA HAS **PAID BACK** THE MONEY WITH PROOF OF PAYMENT.

... ALTHOUGH YOU MIGHT NOT BE **AWARE** OF IT.

I'M ACTUALLY WORKING **HARD**, ALTHOUGH YOU MIGHT NOT BE **AWARE** OF IT.

I ALREADY **PAID** YOU THIS **MONTH**, ALTHOUGH YOU MIGHT NOT BE **AWARE** OF IT.

© RAPID PHASE 2016

I'VE ALREADY **HANDED IN** MY **HOMEWORK**! ... ALTHOUGH YOU MIGHT NOT BE **AWARE** OF IT.

THE **ROADS** HAVE BEEN **FIXED**, ALTHOUGH YOU MIGHT NOT BE **AWARE** OF IT.

IT'S NOW A **BETTER** LIFE FOR **ALL** ... ALTHOUGH YOU MIGHT NOT BE **AWARE** OF IT.

BUT MISTER PRESIDENT... YOU **ARE** A CRIMINAL...

... ALTHOUGH **YOU** MIGHT NOT BE **AWARE** OF IT.

AND IN OTHER NEWS, **PRESIDENT ZUMA** HAS DECIDED THAT 27 DECEMBER WILL BE A NEW "BONUS" **PUBLIC HOLIDAY** THIS YEAR.

ALTHOUGH THE PRESIDENT HASN'T **DECIDED** ON WHAT THE NEW HOLIDAY WILL BE ...

... SOURCES SAY IT'S BETWEEN "NATIONAL NEPOTISM DAY"... "GOODWILL TO GUPTAS DAY..."

... OR "NATIONAL PARDON YOUR PRESIDENT DAY."

NICE TRY.

I THINK DONALD TRUMP IS REALLY ON TO SOMETHING.

UH-OH.

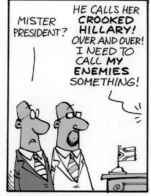

MISTER PRESIDENT?

HE CALLS HER **CROOKED HILLARY!** OVER AND OVER! I NEED TO CALL MY **ENEMIES** SOMETHING!

"CLUELESS PRAVIN!" ..."BIG MOUTH MALEMA!"

SIR... **ORIGINALITY** IS ALWAYS **BETTER.**

GOOD **THINKING!** "ORIGINALITY PRAVIN!" "ORIGINALITY MALEMA!"

YOU TELL HIM.

MISTER PRESIDENT... **PEOPLE** ARE SAYING YOU NEED TO **STEP** DOWN!

I'M **AWARE** OF THE **PROBLEM!** ...AND I HAVE THE PERFECT SOLUTION!

WHAT'S **THAT** SIR?

I'M GOING TO **DOUBLE DOWN!** ...BE EVEN **MORE** SELF-CENTERED! ...SPEND EVEN **MORE** MONEY THAT ISN'T **MINE!**

... AND SAY EVEN **MORE** OF WHATEVER I **WANT** TO, EVEN THOUGH I **KNOW** IT'S ABSOLUTELY **NOT TRUE!**

...YOU'VE BEEN WATCHING **TRUMP** AGAIN, HAVEN'T YOU, SIR?

HUGE! IT'S GOING TO BE **HUGE!**

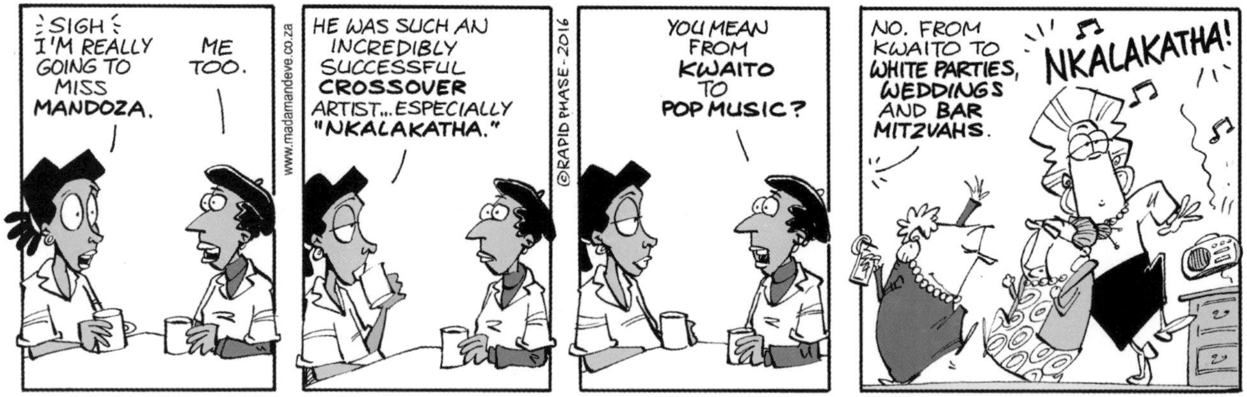
SIGH I'M REALLY GOING TO MISS MANDOZA.
ME TOO.
HE WAS SUCH AN INCREDIBLY SUCCESSFUL CROSSOVER ARTIST... ESPECIALLY "NKALAKATHA."
www.madamandeve.co.za
©RAPID PHASE-2016
YOU MEAN FROM KWAITO TO POP MUSIC?
NO. FROM KWAITO TO WHITE PARTIES, WEDDINGS AND BAR MITZVAHS.
NKALAKATHA!

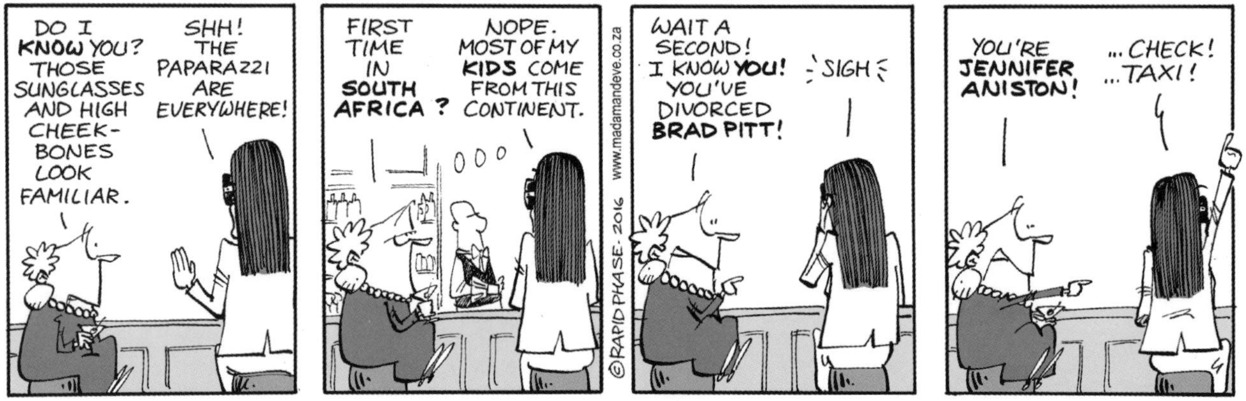
DO I KNOW YOU? THOSE SUNGLASSES AND HIGH CHEEK-BONES LOOK FAMILIAR.
SHH! THE PAPARAZZI ARE EVERYWHERE!
FIRST TIME IN SOUTH AFRICA?
NOPE. MOST OF MY KIDS COME FROM THIS CONTINENT.
www.madamandeve.co.za
©RAPID PHASE-2016
WAIT A SECOND! I KNOW YOU! YOU'VE DIVORCED BRAD PITT!
SIGH
YOU'RE JENNIFER ANISTON!
...CHECK! ...TAXI!

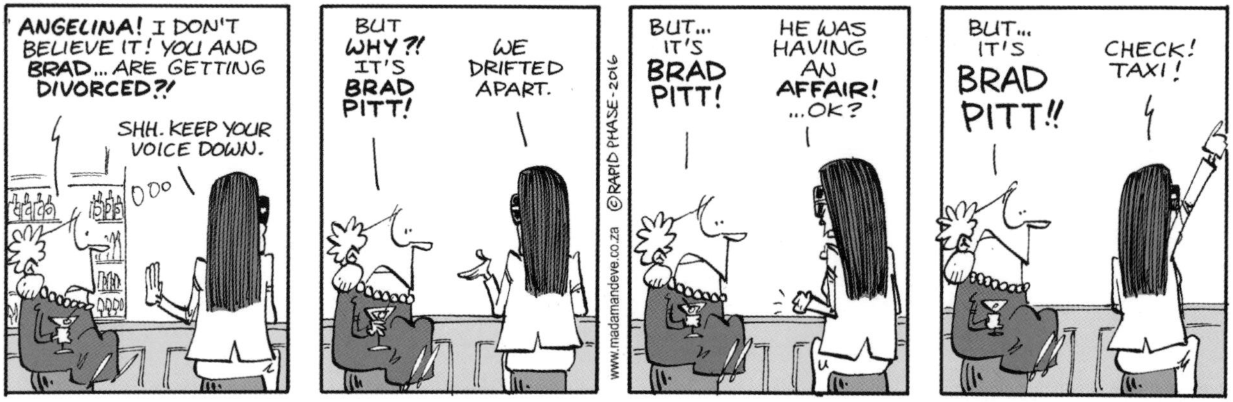
ANGELINA! I DON'T BELIEVE IT! YOU AND BRAD... ARE GETTING DIVORCED?!
SHH. KEEP YOUR VOICE DOWN.
BUT WHY?! IT'S BRAD PITT!
WE DRIFTED APART.
©RAPID PHASE-2016
www.madamandeve.co.za
BUT... IT'S BRAD PITT!
HE WAS HAVING AN AFFAIR! ...OK?
BUT... IT'S BRAD PITT!!
CHECK! TAXI!

TAG! YOU'RE IT!!

I REFUSE TO ACCEPT THAT I'M "IT"! I'M TAKING THE MATTER TO THE CONSTITUTIONAL COURT!

GO AHEAD! I'LL APPEAL!

GO AHEAD AND APPEAL! I'LL IGNORE THE RULING EVEN IF YOU WIN!

WANNA PLAY AGAIN?

OKAY!

"TAG" USED TO BE A LOT SIMPLER WHEN I WAS A KID.

WHEN I GROW UP I'M GOING TO WORK IN GOVERNMENT.

SERVING THE PEOPLE?

NO. I WANT TO HIRE MY FRIENDS, SPEND TAXPAYER'S MONEY... AND RIDE IN LIMOS WITH FLASHING BLUE LIGHTS!

... NOT ALL GOVERNMENT OFFICIALS DO THAT!

I KNOW! SOME GET SUSPENDED AND GET TO STAY HOME DOING NOTHING AND GET PAID FOR IT!

VISUALISING CAREER GOALS IS ALWAYS IMPORTANT.

UP NEXT ON SABC...

... IT'S "KEEPING UP WITH HLAUDI!" ON TONIGHT'S EPISODE ...

... AFTER BEING REMOVED BY THE SUPREME COURT OF APPEAL, HLAUDI DECIDES TO APPLY FOR HIS OLD JOB AT THE SABC. HILARITY ENSUES!

NEW SITCOM?

REALITY TV.

CAN YOU HELP ME WITH MY **HISTORY HOMEWORK?**

≥SIGH≥ OKAY. GO AHEAD.

NAME AN **ANCIENT** LEADER AND A **MODERN** ONE THAT CAUSED MANY BATTLES AND **CONFLICTS.**

LET'S SEE... **ALEXANDER** THE **GREAT,** 356 **B.C.**

...AND **HLAUDI** THE **GRATING,** S.A.B.C.

MOM!!

RiPLEY'S~ Believe It or Not!

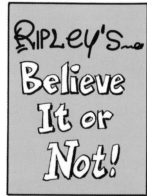

WOLFGANG AMADEUS MOZART

LEARNED TO PLAY HIS FIRST INSTRUMENT, THE HAPSICHORD, AT THE AGE OF **THREE!**

UK WINE CONSULTANT **PHILIP OSENTON** CAN HOLD **FIFTY** WINE GLASSES IN **ONE HAND** ... AT THE **SAME TIME!**

DESPITE **INSANE** UTTERANCES, FAKED QUALIFICATIONS, **LOSSES** OF **400 MILLION...** AND HAVING HIS POSITION AS COO **SET ASIDE** BY THE SUPREME COURT OF APPEAL, **HLAUDI MOTSOENENG** IS **STILL EMPLOYED** BY THE **SABC!**

From the makers of Hyundai... comes a new car that just won't quit.

Even though everybody wants it to.

INTRODUCING... THE NEW HLAUDI

"It works miracles!"

"Unstoppable!"

"90% local content!"

Goes from 0 - 11.4 million in under 60 seconds.

Let Hlaudi take you for a ride!

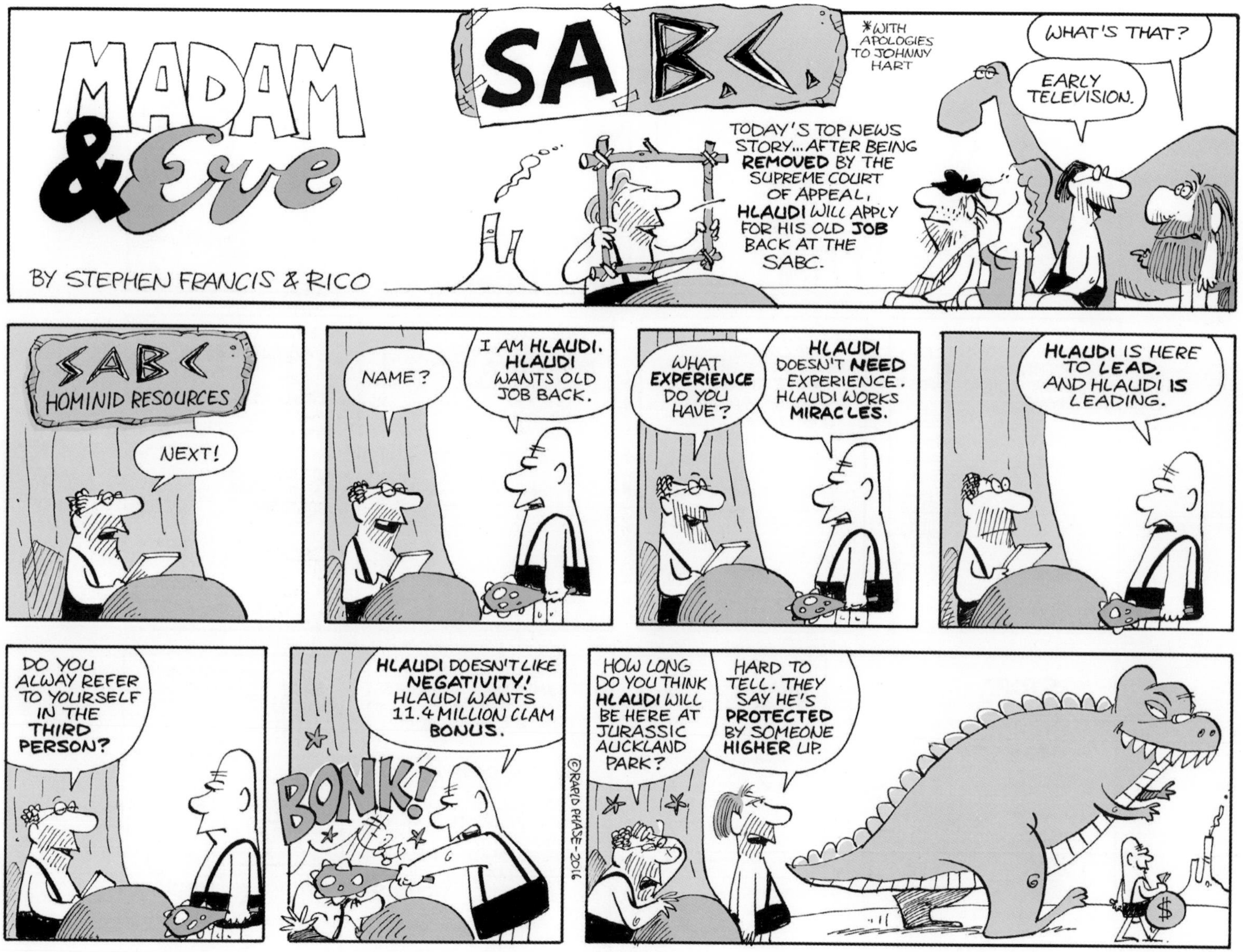
MADAM & Eve
BY STEPHEN FRANCIS & RICO
SABC
*WITH APOLOGIES TO JOHNNY HART
WHAT'S THAT?
EARLY TELEVISION.
TODAY'S TOP NEWS STORY... AFTER BEING REMOVED BY THE SUPREME COURT OF APPEAL, HLAUDI WILL APPLY FOR HIS OLD JOB BACK AT THE SABC.
SABC HOMINID RESOURCES
NEXT!
NAME?
I AM HLAUDI. HLAUDI WANTS OLD JOB BACK.
WHAT EXPERIENCE DO YOU HAVE?
HLAUDI DOESN'T NEED EXPERIENCE. HLAUDI WORKS MIRACLES.
HLAUDI IS HERE TO LEAD. AND HLAUDI IS LEADING.
DO YOU ALWAY REFER TO YOURSELF IN THE THIRD PERSON?
HLAUDI DOESN'T LIKE NEGATIVITY! HLAUDI WANTS 11.4 MILLION CLAM BONUS.
BONK!
©RAPID PHASE-2016
HOW LONG DO YOU THINK HLAUDI WILL BE HERE AT JURASSIC AUCKLAND PARK?
HARD TO TELL. THEY SAY HE'S PROTECTED BY SOMEONE HIGHER UP.
$

Plink!

Plink!

#PEAS MUSTFALL.

EVERYBODY SEEMS SO **SERIOUS** THESE DAYS.

IS EVERYTHING ALRIGHT, MISTER PRESIDENT?

HAVE YOU SEEN THE **HEADLINES**?!

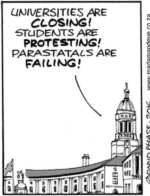

UNIVERSITIES ARE **CLOSING**! STUDENTS ARE **PROTESTING**! PARASTATALS ARE **FAILING**!

THE SABC IS **REBELLING**! DONALD TRUMP IS **BRAGGING**!

YOUR POINT, SIR?

EVERYONE'S **FORGOTTEN** ABOUT **ME**!

I GET **NERVOUS** WHEN HE'S THIS HAPPY.

STOP! YOU'RE UNDER ARREST!!

WHAT AM I BEING CHARGED WITH?

CORRUPTION!

BAH! THOSE ARE JUST **TRUMPED UP** CHARGES TO FACILITATE **STATE CAPTURE**!

HOW **DARE** YOU IMPLY **POLITICAL INTERFERENCE** IN OUR INDEPENDENT PROSECUTION?!

SEE YOU IN COURT!

SEE YOU IN COURT!

WHATEVER HAPPENED TO JUST PLAYING "**COPS** AND **ROBBERS**"?

MADAM & Eve

BY STEPHEN FRANCIS & RICO

HELLO. I'M YOUR NEW CABIN ATTENDANT, DUDU MYENI.

AS CHAIRPERSON OF DEBT-RIDDEN SAA WITH **BILLIONS** OF RANDS OF **LOSSES**, I'VE DECIDED TO DO VARIOUS JOBS **MYSELF** SO I CAN BETTER **UNDERSTAND** HOW AN AIRLINE ACTUALLY **WORKS**.

THE **EXITS** ARE LOCATED... WELL, I'M NOT TOO **SURE**... SINCE **DOORS** ARE USUALLY **OPENED** FOR ME!

PLEASE KEEP YOUR **SEATBELTS** FASTENED, IN CASE WE ENCOUNTER HEAVY **FLATULENCE**.

AND, IF **CABINET PRESSURE** SHOULD DROP, THESE LITTLE **YELLOW** THINGIES WILL DROP FROM THE **CEILING**.

IN THE UNLIKELY EVENT OF AN EMERGENCY **WATER** LANDING, DON'T BLAME ME, BECAUSE I **INHERITED** ALL THESE **PROBLEMS**...

... OTHERWISE YOU CAN BLAME APARTHEID.

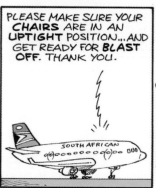

PLEASE MAKE SURE YOUR **CHAIRS** ARE IN AN **UPTIGHT** POSITION... AND GET READY FOR **BLAST OFF**. THANK YOU.

© RAPID PHASE - 2016

THIS IS **CAPTAIN** DUDU MYENI SPEAKING. WE'LL BE FLYING AT A REALLY HIGH **LONGITUDE**...

MR. ABRAHAMS! WERE YOU PRESSURED BY PRESIDENT ZUMA TO BRING CHARGES AGAINST FINANCE MINISTER GORDHAN?

ABSOLUTELY NOT!

AND YOU WILL SEE THAT PRAVIN GORDHAN IS GUILTY AS SOON AS OUR FALSE WITNESS TESTIFIES!

: AHEM : PSST. B222. B222.

FIRST WITNESS! AS SOON AS OUR FIRST WITNESS TESTIFIES!

IN OTHER NEWS, PRESIDENT ZUMA HAS OBJECTED TO THE PUBLIC PROTECTOR'S STATE CAPTURE INVESTIGATION AND DEMANDS TO QUESTION ALL WITNESSES HIMSELF!

TELL ME... DID YOU EVER ACTUALLY SEE ME CONSPIRING WITH THE GUPTAS? REMEMBER-- YOU'RE UNDER OATH!

YES. I SAW YOU.

THEN PERHAPS YOU CAN TELL US HOW YOU SAW ME... WHEN YOU WEREN'T... WEARING YOUR GLASSES!

UH, I DON'T WEAR GLASSES!

LUNCH BREAK!!

THIS JUST IN... PRESIDENT ZUMA DEMANDS TO PERSONALLY CROSS-EXAMINE ALL WITNESSES IN THE PUBLIC PROTECTOR'S STATE CAPTURE INVESTIGATION!

SO YOU "CLAIM" YOU SAW ME CONSPIRING WITH THE GUPTA BROTHERS ON MARCH 25th.

YES.

MAYBE THIS WILL REFRESH YOUR MEMORY! THIS ALMANAC PROVES THERE WAS NO MOON THAT NIGHT! HOW COULD YOU HAVE SEEN ME?!

IT WAS DURING THE DAYTIME.

RECESS!

MADAM & Eve

BY STEPHEN FRANCIS & RICO

COMING UP... MORE **NEWS** ABOUT EVERYONE'S FAVOURITE WACKY "ORDINARY EMPLOYEE" AT THE **SABC**, HLAUDI MOTSOENENG!

≥SIGH.≥

ENOUGH ALREADY!!

≥Click!≥

I'M CALLING A MORATORIUM! NO MORE **HLAUDI** JOKES... UNTIL **SOMEONE** IN GOVERNMENT **DOES** SOMETHING ABOUT THIS SITUATION!!

THIS JUST IN...

≥Click!≥

HLAUDI MOTSOENENG HAS BEEN **REMOVED** FROM THE **SABC!**

FINALLY!

... AND HAS BEEN **REDEPLOYED** AS THE NEW **MINISTER** OF HIGHER EDUCATION!

CRASH!!

©RAPID PHASE·2016

ATTENTION! THE FIRST STUDENT THAT **RETURNS** TO CLASS, GETS HLAUDI'S NEW **HAT!**

FEES MUST FALL

FREE EDUCATION

NO! DON'T **TRUST HIM!** IT'S A **TRICK!!**

I THOUGHT I TOLD YOU TO **WATER DOWN** HER DRINKS.

THERE'S A **WATER** SHORTAGE.

MISTER PRESIDENT?

YES! YES! YES! YES!

HAPPY DAYS ARE HERE AGAIN!!

WHAT'S GOING ON?

FWEEP!

WOOHOO! BWAHAHA!!

THULI MADONSELA'S TERM AS PUBLIC PROTECTOR HAS ENDED.

SHOUT IT FROM THE ROOFTOPS! I'M FREE OF HER AT LAST!

YOU HAVEN'T TOLD HIM ABOUT PRAVIN GORDHAN'S "GUPTA" AFFADAVIT?

NOT YET.

IT'S THE FIGHT OF THE DECADE ZUMA VS GORDHAN! LET'S GET READY TO RUMBLE -DING! AND THERE'S THE BELL!

... AND ZUMA LEADS WITH A FRAUD CHARGE, FOLLOWED BY A LOW BLOW TO GORDHAN'S JUNK STATUS!

BUT GORDHAN COMES BACK! IT'S A PUNISHING RIGHT TO THE AFFADAVIT!

ZUMA'S IN TROUBLE!

THERE'S RAPID FIRE JABS TO THE GUPTA! ZUMA'S ON THE ROPES!

EVE!! MORE POPCORN!!

AND SO... THE GIANT, OVERSIZED FORCES OF STATE CAPTURE TRIED TO CRUSH PRAVIN.

BUT PRAVIN WAS CLEVER AND PRESENTED A COURT APPLICATION THAT QUICKLY DEFEATED THEM.

CRASH!

THE END.

WHAT KIND OF A CRAZY STORY IS THAT?!

"AFFIDAVIT AND GOLIATH."

THANDI! WHERE'S YOUR HOMEWORK?!

SOMEBODY **STOLE** IT!!

THE WHOLE THING IS **RIGGED!** THE ENTIRE MEDIA'S **AGAINST** ME! IT'S A **ROGUE** UNIT! A **HUGE** CONSPIRACY!!

YOU GOT THAT FROM **DONALD TRUMP,** RIGHT?

ACTUALLY... I GOT IT FROM **JACOB ZUMA...** HLAUDI MOTSOENENG, GWEDE MANTASHE, THE GUPTAS...

© RAPID PHASE - 2016

www.madamandeve.co.za

FAMOUS MELTDOWNS THROUGH HISTORY

THE WICKED WITCH OF THE WEST

I'M MELTING! **MELTING!!**

CHERNOBYL

EVACUATE!

SHE'S GONNA **BLOW!!**

TRUMP

IT'S **RIGGED!** THE ELECTION IS RIGGED! IT'S A CONSPIRACY!!

© RAPID PHASE - 2016

www.madamandeve.co.za

AAAAH!!

PLOP!!

MAYBE I NEED TO **RETHINK** THIS YEAR'S **HALLOWEEN** COSTUME.

© RAPID PHASE - 2016

www.madamandeve.co.za

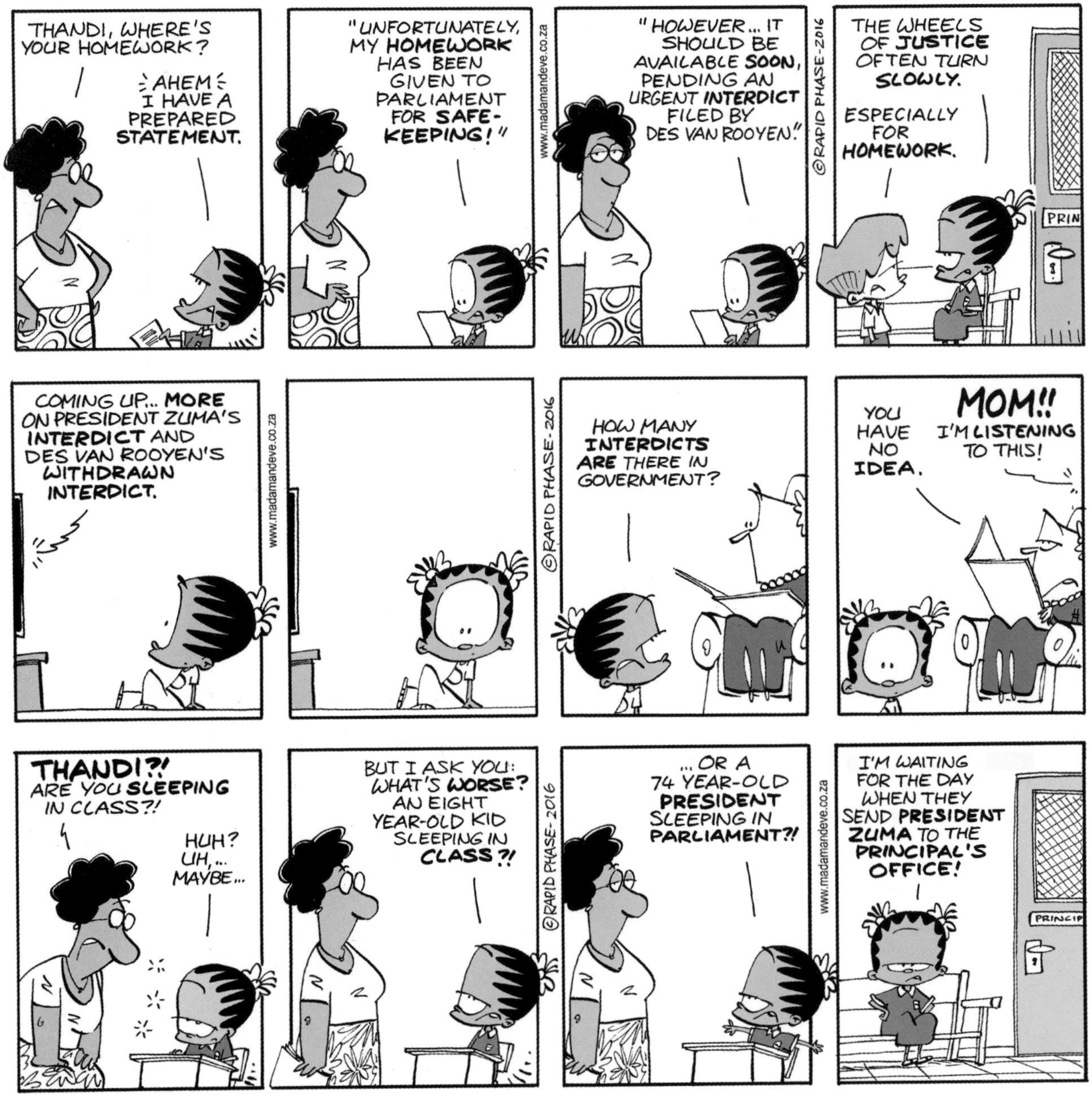
THANDI, WHERE'S YOUR HOMEWORK?
AHEM I HAVE A PREPARED STATEMENT.
"UNFORTUNATELY, MY HOMEWORK HAS BEEN GIVEN TO PARLIAMENT FOR SAFE-KEEPING!"
www.madamandeve.co.za
"HOWEVER... IT SHOULD BE AVAILABLE SOON, PENDING AN URGENT INTERDICT FILED BY DES VAN ROOYEN."
© RAPID PHASE - 2016
THE WHEELS OF JUSTICE OFTEN TURN SLOWLY.
ESPECIALLY FOR HOMEWORK.
PRIN
COMING UP... MORE ON PRESIDENT ZUMA'S INTERDICT AND DES VAN ROOYEN'S WITHDRAWN INTERDICT.
www.madamandeve.co.za
© RAPID PHASE - 2016
HOW MANY INTERDICTS ARE THERE IN GOVERNMENT?
YOU HAVE NO IDEA.
MOM!! I'M LISTENING TO THIS!
THANDI?! ARE YOU SLEEPING IN CLASS?!
HUH? UH,... MAYBE...
BUT I ASK YOU: WHAT'S WORSE? AN EIGHT YEAR-OLD KID SLEEPING IN CLASS?!
© RAPID PHASE - 2016
...OR A 74 YEAR-OLD PRESIDENT SLEEPING IN PARLIAMENT?!
www.madamandeve.co.za
I'M WAITING FOR THE DAY WHEN THEY SEND PRESIDENT ZUMA TO THE PRINCIPAL'S OFFICE!
PRINCIP

MADAM & Eve

BY STEPHEN FRANCIS & RICO.

I'M NOT SURE I UNDERSTAND THIS WHOLE "FEES MUST FALL" THING.

WELL, THEY SAY IT BEGAN IN THE TIME OF JACOB... THERE AROSE A NEW STUDENT LEADER...

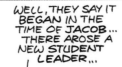

...NAMED MOSES. HE LED THE EXODUS TO FREE HIS PEOPLE FROM EDUCATIONAL FINANCIAL BONDAGE!

NOW, MOSES HAD ALREADY SEEN MANY THINGS. HE WAS THERE WHEN THE RED SEA PARTED IN PARLIAMENT.

PAY BACK THE MONEY! PAY BACK THE MONEY!

© RAPID PHASE · 2016

THEN MOSES WENT TO THE CAMPUSES AND SAID:

LET MY PEOPLE GO! ...BACK TO UNIVERSITY FOR FREE!

BUT THE MINISTER OF HIGHER EDUCATION'S HEART WAS HARDENED. ...AND HE SAID <u>NO</u>!

SO MOSES BROUGHT DOWN UPON HIM A TERRIBLE PLAGUE... OF HASHTAGS, STONES AND FIRE.

#FEES MUST FALL

AND THE STUDENTS DEMONSTRATED FOR FORTY DAYS... AND FORTY NIGHTS.

POLICE

WAIT A MINUTE! HOW DID MOSES KNOW TO DO ALL THIS?

SIMPLE. HE SAW A SIGN...

...THE BURNING BUS.

MOM! THAT'S ENOUGH!!

THIS ALL SOUNDS VERY FAMILIAR.

THOU SHALT NOT INTERRUPT MY STORY!

Panel 1: MISTER PRESIDENT! WOULD YOU CARE TO COMMENT ON THE **STATE CAPTURE** INVESTIGATION?

YES! I'M TOTALLY **INNOCENT!**

Panel 2: ... AND IF YOU DON'T BELIEVE ME, JUST **ASK** SOME OF MY **SUPPORTERS!** ... LIKE THE ANC **LOOT LEAGUE!**

Panel 3: ≶ AHEM ≶ PSST. B222. B222.

Panel 4: **YOUTH** LEAGUE!! THE ANC **YOUTH LEAGUE!**

Panel 5: THANDI -- DO YOU HAVE YOUR **HOMEWORK**, OR **NOT**?!

NO -- BUT IT'S **NOT** MY **FAULT!**

Panel 6: I WAS HELD **HOSTAGE** BY THE **HAWKS** AT THE **SARS** OFFICES!

Panel 7: ... AND THEY WOULDN'T LET YOU **OUT** UNTIL YOU **GAVE UP** YOUR **HOMEWORK** DOCUMENT?

YES!! HOW DID YOU **KNOW?!**

Panel 8: ... SHE'S OBVIOUSLY **PART OF THE CONSPIRACY.**

PRINCI

Panel 9: AND WE'LL BE RIGHT **BACK** ... WITH MORE ON **ZUMA'S** STATE CAPTURE REPORT INTERDICT, THE FEES MUST FALL CRISIS, AND THE FALL-OUT FROM THE PRAVIN GORDHAN **CHARGES.**

Panel 10: WITH **ALL** THIS GOING ON, HOW DOES PRESIDENT ZUMA HAVE **TIME** TO **RUN THE COUNTRY?**

HE HAS **HELPERS.**

Panel 11: YOU MEAN LIKE FATHER CHRISTMAS HAS LITTLE **ELVES?**

YES. THEY HELP **RUN** THINGS WHEN HE'S **BUSY.**

Panel 12: LIKE **WHO?**

LITTLE **AJAY** AND **ATUL.**

MOM!

32

MADAM & Eve

BY STEPHEN FRANCIS & RICO

AN ELITE UNIT.

IT'S GOING **DOWN**! WE HAVE EYES ON THE SUSPECT! LET'S **MOVE**!

READY FOR ACTION!

ANYTIME, ANYWHERE.

ATTENTION UNITS! USE CAUTION! UNDERCOVER OFFICER ON SCENE!

ROGER THAT!

©RAPID PHASE · 2016

THEY ALWAYS GET THEIR MAN... OR WOMAN.

WE CAN DO THIS THE **EASY** WAY... OR THE **HARD** WAY. IT'S UP TO YOU.

FREEZE! YOU'RE UNDER ARREST!

DROP THAT HOSEPIPE! ...AND KICK IT OVER HERE!

SPRINKLER SQUAD

WATER RESTRICTION POLICE

Coming soon to SABC 3

THEY'RE REALLY GETTING DESPERATE FOR LOCAL CONTENT.

R.C.

Row 1

NOVEMBER 5: WE BEGIN OUR **EXPEDITION** AT SUNRISE.

FAILURE IS **NOT** AN OPTION...

OUR MAP: HASTILY SCRIBBLED DIRECTIONS ON A **TEAR-STAINED** BEER COASTER... BY AN EXPLORER NAMED "MOLEFE."

WHAT WILL WE FIND? ARE THE MYTHS AND LEGENDS **TRUE?!**

DOES IT REALLY **EXIST?**

JOIN US...AS WE CONTINUE OUR PERILOUS JOURNEY...

THE SEARCH FOR THE LOST SHEBEEN OF SAXONWOLD

Row 2

IS MISTER ABRAHAMS HERE?

GO RIGHT IN.

NPA

SHAUN! ARE YOU AWARE THAT CARTOONISTS ARE CALLING YOU "**SHAUN THE SHEEP**"?

YES.

WELL? WHAT DO YOU HAVE TO **SAY** ABOUT IT?

BAH!

Row 3

EVE'S TEACHING A **YOGA** AND **MEDITATION** CLASS FOR THE NEIGHBOURHOOD DOMESTIC WORKERS.

ARE THOSE THEIR **YOGA MATS?**

...NOT EXACTLY.

RIGHT, LET'S BEGIN WITH THE "**STINGY MADAM.**" BREATHE...1...2...3...4...

MADAM & Eve

BY STEPHEN FRANCIS & RICO

AND IN OTHER NEWS... CERTAIN **GOVERNMENT OFFICIALS** STILL MAINTAIN THAT THEY **MAY** HAVE VISITED A **SHEBEEN** WHICH COINCIDENTALLY, IS LOCATED **NEAR** THE GUPTA'S **SAXONWOLD** RESIDENCE.

HAVE YOU SEEN MY MOTHER?

NO. ...WHY?

SO THIS IS THE FAMOUS **SAXONWOLD** SHEBEEN. I'LL HAVE A GIN & TONIC.

COMING UP.

THAT'S ODD... SOME KIND OF **TRAPDOOR** BEHIND THE BAR.

©RAPID PHASE 2016

HELLO. ARE YOU HERE FOR THE **FINANCE MINISTER** POSITION?

I KNEW IT!!

SHAUN THE SHEEP

GUPTA THE GOAT

HLAUDI THE HYENA

MOLEFE THE CRYING MAMBA

SOUTH AFRICAN PETTING ZOO

ZUMA THE ZEBRA

CURRENTLY IN ZIMBABWE

HISS!

SNIFF!

THEY DON'T LOOK **FRIENDLY** AT ALL.

AS I WAS SAYING, I'M TOTALLY **INNOCENT** OF **STATE CAPTURE**. I'LL FIGHT THE CHARGES UNTIL THE END.

...WE... ER, ADMIRE YOUR **CONVICTION**, MISTER PRESIDENT.

WHAT "CONVICTION?!" NOTHING HAS BEEN **PROVEN** YET!

UH... FURTHERMORE, I DEMAND MY **DELAY** IN COURT!

DAY IN COURT! I DEMAND MY **DAY** IN COURT!

©RAPID PHASE-2016   www.madamandeve.co.za

AND IN OTHER NEWS... CHANNEL ANN 7'S "SOUTH AFRICAN OF THE YEAR" AWARDS HAVE BEEN POSTPONED.

AWWWW.

©RAPID PHASE-2016

THE **GUPTAS** COULDN'T DECIDE BETWEEN **PRESIDENT ZUMA, SHAUN ABRAHAMS**...

www.madamandeve.co.za

...OR **DES VAN ROOYEN**.

CRASH!

MADAM & Eve

BY STEPHEN FRANCIS & RICO

MOTHER ANDERSON'S
SAXONWOLD SHEBEEN
DESIGNER COCKTAILS MENU

POINT OF ORDER

(AKA *THE POPULIST*) RED BULL, RED BULL, RED BULL, MORE RED BULL. EVEN MORE RED BULL. DRINK SEVERAL, THEN THROW YOURSELF OUT OF THE SHEBEEN AND OCCUPY A WHITE PERSON'S PARKING SPACE.

MOLEFE MARTINI

(AKA *SAXONWOLD SUNRISE*) SCHNAPPS, RUM, BITTERS, ESSENCE OF CROCODILE TEARS. DRINK 3 AND THEN DESTROY YOUR CELLPHONE. QUIT YOUR HIGH-PAYING PARASTATAL JOB.

BLOODY HLAUDI

VODKA, TOMATO JUICE, 90% LOCAL CONTENT. DRINK WHILE PAYING YOUR TV LICENCE & SHOUT: "BLOODY HLAUDI!"

SPIN DOCTOR

SYNTHETIC ETHANOL ALCOHOL, SNAKE OIL, ABSINTHE. DRINK TWO OF THESE AND YOU'LL BELIEVE ANYTHING.

THE NUKE

QUADRUPLE IMPORTED RUSSIAN VODKA. DRINK IN SECRET. TAKE OUT MASSIVE LOAN TO KEEP BUYING FOR YOUR FRIENDS UNTIL BANKRUPT.

STATE CAPTURE

WHISKY, RUM, VODKA, SLICEOF LIME, A PINCH OF CURRY POWDER. DRINK TWO AND YOU'LL ACCEPT ANY MINISTERIAL POSITION OFFERED.

ZUMA ZOMBIE

IMPORTED SCOTCH, BITTER LEMON, SOUR GRAPES, A SHOT OF FIREPOOL WATER. SEND BILL TO THE TAXPAYER. "HEH. HEH. HEH."

DONALD TRUMP'S MEXICAN WALLBANGER

TREMENDOUS VODKA, UNBELIEVABLE TEQUILA, BEST-EVER BOURBON INCREDIBLE VERMOUTH, AMAZING CHAMPAGNE (SERVE IN A *HUUGE* GOLD-RIMMED GLASS WITH A SWINDLE STICK)

GREAT WALL OF CHINA

GREAT WALL OF TRUMP

GREAT WALL OF ZUMA

ALL THOSE **AGAINST** THE "MOTION OF NO CONFIDENCE" IN PRESIDENT ZUMA"...

"QUESTION #4..."

"GIVE TWO EXAMPLES OF A **CHOKING HAZARD**."

" 1) THE HONOURABLE JACOB ZUMA...
2) PRESIDENT-ELECT TRUMP "

THE TRIBE HAS SPOKEN.

©RAPID PHASE - 2016 www.madamandeve.co.za

...ER, IF THERE WAS A TRIBE LEFT TO SPEAK OF.

SABC BOARD

SURVIVOR

Now on SABC 1,2 & 3

TALK ABOUT TAKING REALITY TV TO A WHOLE NEW LEVEL.

EVERYONE? OPPOSITION PARTIES ARE DEMANDING THAT ALL CORRUPT MINISTERS FOLLOW ESKOM CEO BRIAN MOLEFE'S BOLD EXAMPLE.

www.madamandeve.co.za

WELL, IT'S NOT GOING TO BE EASY... BUT I SAY WE GIVE IN AND DO EXACTLY WHAT BRIAN MOLEFE DID. AGREED?

AGREED!

:SIGH: I'LL GO FIRST. OK -- I ADMIT IT! I WAS... AT THE SHEBEEN!

ME TOO!

ME ALSO!

I'VE BEEN SPENDING LOTS OF TIME THERE!

LOOK! :SOB: I'M EVEN CRYING!

DO WE ALL HAVE TO CRY?

©RAPID PHASE - 2016

OPPOSITION PARTIES AND PEOPLE EVERYWHERE HAVE SUGGESTED THAT I FOLLOW THE EXAMPLE OF ESKOM CEO BRIAN MOLEFE.

I HAVE DECIDED TO TAKE THEIR ADVICE!

:GASP: Y-YOU'RE STEPPING DOWN, MISTER PRESIDENT?!

www.madamandeve.co.za

NO. BUT I'VE DECIDED TO ADMIT I'VE SPENT LOTS OF TIME IN THE SAXONWOLD SHEBEEN.

©RAPID PHASE - 2016

EVE! ANOTHER GIN & TONIC! MAKE IT A DOUBLE!

39

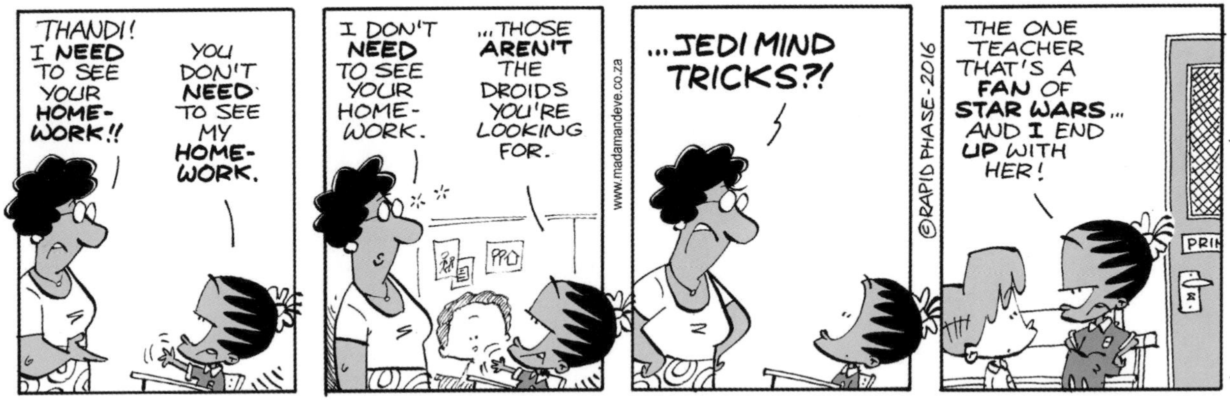
THANDI! I NEED TO SEE YOUR HOME-WORK!!
YOU DON'T NEED TO SEE MY HOME-WORK.
I DON'T NEED TO SEE YOUR HOME-WORK.
...THOSE AREN'T THE DROIDS YOU'RE LOOKING FOR.
www.madamandeve.co.za
...JEDI MIND TRICKS?!
©RAPID PHASE-2016
THE ONE TEACHER THAT'S A FAN OF STAR WARS... AND I END UP WITH HER!
PRI

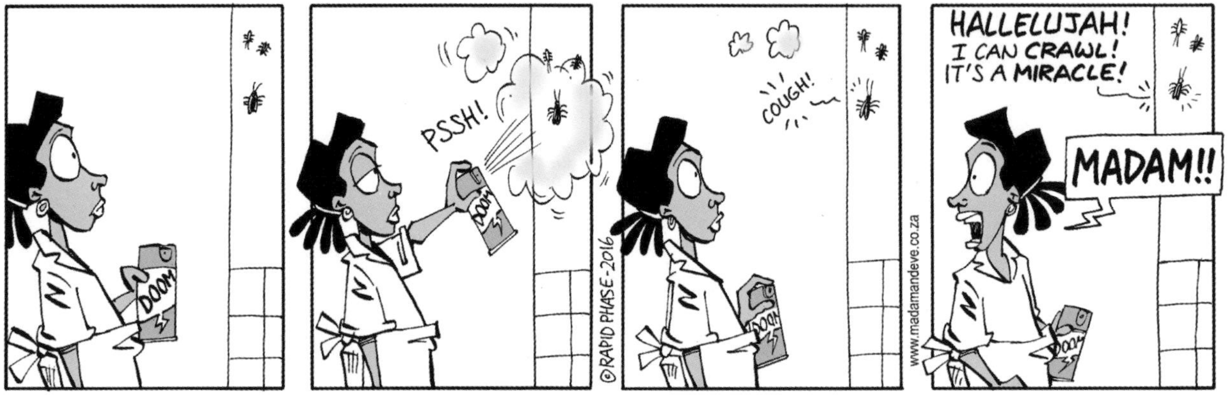
DOOM
PSSH!
DOOM
©RAPID PHASE-2016
COUGH!
DOOM
HALLELUJAH! I CAN CRAWL! IT'S A MIRACLE!
MADAM!!
www.madamandeve.co.za

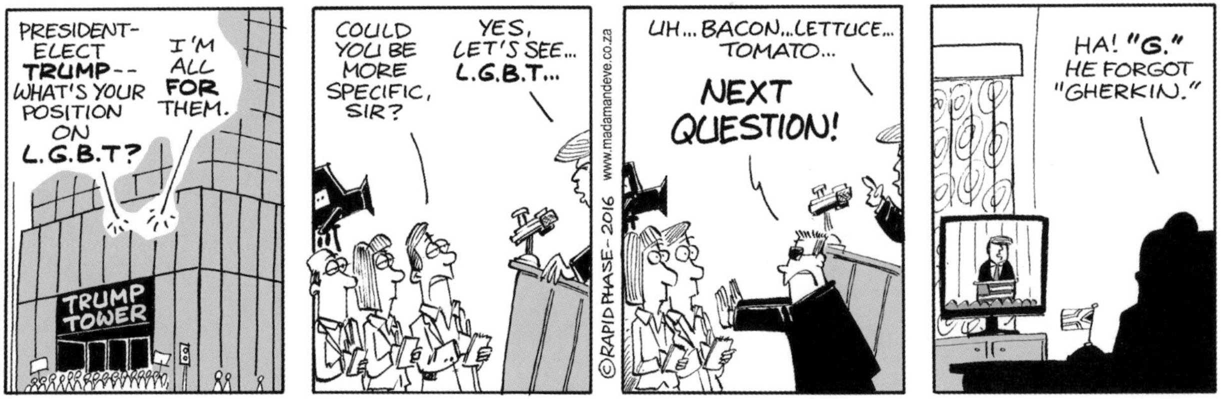
PRESIDENT-ELECT TRUMP-- WHAT'S YOUR POSITION ON L.G.B.T?
I'M ALL FOR THEM.
TRUMP TOWER
COULD YOU BE MORE SPECIFIC, SIR?
YES, LET'S SEE... L.G.B.T...
www.madamandeve.co.za
©RAPID PHASE-2016
UH... BACON...LETTUCE... TOMATO...
NEXT QUESTION!
HA! "G." HE FORGOT "GHERKIN."

MADAM & Eve

BY STEPHEN FRANCIS & RICO

GO ON.

I DON'T KNOW, DOCTOR. I CAN'T SEEM TO GET **MOTIVATED**. I FEEL LIKE A **FAILURE**.

I CAN'T SEEM TO GET MY **HEAD** IN THE **GAME**.

REMEMBER... "DO NOT JUDGE ME BY MY **SUCCESSES**. JUDGE ME BY HOW MANY **TIMES** I GET BACK **UP** AGAIN."

THAT'S GREAT! WHO SAID **THAT?!**

NELSON MANDELA.

"I DON'T KNOW THE **KEY** TO **SUCCESS**... BUT THE KEY TO **FAILURE** IS TRYING TO **PLEASE** EVERYBODY."

FANTASTIC! WHO SAID **THAT?!**

UH... BILL COSBY.

≥GROAN!≤

ER... I SEE YOUR **TIME** IS UP.

≥SIGH≤ I'LL PAY YOU FOR THE MONTH. **TOSS** ME MY **WALLET.**

HERE YOU GO. CATCH!

©RAPID PHASE - 2016

OOPS! OOPS! OOPS!

OOPS! ≥TRIP!≤ OOPS! CLATTER! **CRASH!!** **AAAAH!!**

ER... TELL YOU WHAT... LET'S CALL THIS SESSION **PRO BONO.**

EDITH ANDERSON?

YES.

SIGN HERE FOR DELIVERY.

OKAY GUYS! **BRING IT IN!**

LOVE THOSE **BLACK FRIDAY** SPECIALS.

MOM! LOOK AT **THIS!** WE'RE **OVERDRAWN** AT THE **BANK!**

YOU SPENT FAR TOO MUCH **MONEY** ON **GIN & TONIC** DELIVERIES FOR **BLACK FRIDAY!!**

WELL...THAT'S WHAT COMES **AFTER** BLACK FRIDAY.

... **RED MONDAY.**

AND IN OTHER NEWS... THE **NEW** PUBLIC PROTECTOR HAS ANNOUNCED HER **FIRST** ANTI-CORRUPTION **INVESTIGATION.**

AHA.

SHE SAYS SHE WILL **INVESTIGATE** THE **PREVIOUS** PUBLIC PROTECTOR... WHO HAD ALREADY **INVESTIGATED** CORRUPTION **PREVIOUSLY.**

AAAAAH!!

WHO **KNEW** THAT PUBLIC PROTECTORS NEEDED TO PROTECT THE PUBLIC FROM PUBLIC PROTECTORS.

CAN YOU HELP ME WITH MY ENGLISH GRAMMAR HOMEWORK?

SURE.

"NAME AN EXAMPLE OF AN OXYMORON."

ANC INTEGRITY COMMITTEE.

MOM!!

I AM THE GENIE OF THE LAMP! WHAT ARE YOUR THREE WISHES?

REALLY? I WANT TO BE RICH AND FAMOUS!

... I WANT TO BE POWERFUL!

... I WANT TO BE UNTOUCHABLE AND UNDEFEATED!

YOUR WISHES ARE MY COMMAND!

POOF!

HEH. HEH.

HEH. HEH.

AND I WANT--

YOU'VE ALREADY HAD THREE WISHES.

...I WANT TO BE BETTER AT MATHS.

SLAM!

IT'S SCHOOL HOLIDAYS!!

WHERE'S GOGO?

SHH.

IT'S THE **SILLY SEASON!**

DO YOU THINK ANYONE KEEPS A HISTORICAL **RECORD** OF THE SILLY SEASON?

WHAT DO YOU MEAN?

FOR EXAMPLE, WHEN DID THE SILLY SEASON OFFICIALLY **BEGIN?**

IN **2007**... AT THE **POLOKWANE** ANC NATIONAL **CONFERENCE.**

MOM!!

SANTA

HO HO HO!

ZUMA

HEH. HEH. HEH.

HLAUDI

BWA HA HA HA HA!

SABC

SHAUN

BAA. BAA. BAA.

HI. WE'RE YOUR **DUSTBIN MEN.** WE'RE HERE FOR OUR CHRISTMAS **BONUS.**

HI. WE'RE YOUR **DELIVERY MEN.** WE'RE HERE FOR OUR CHRISTMAS **BONUS.**

HI. WE'RE YOUR **GINGERBREAD MEN.** WE'RE HERE FOR OUR--

SLAM!!

WELL... IT WAS WORTH A **SHOT.**

NICE TRY!

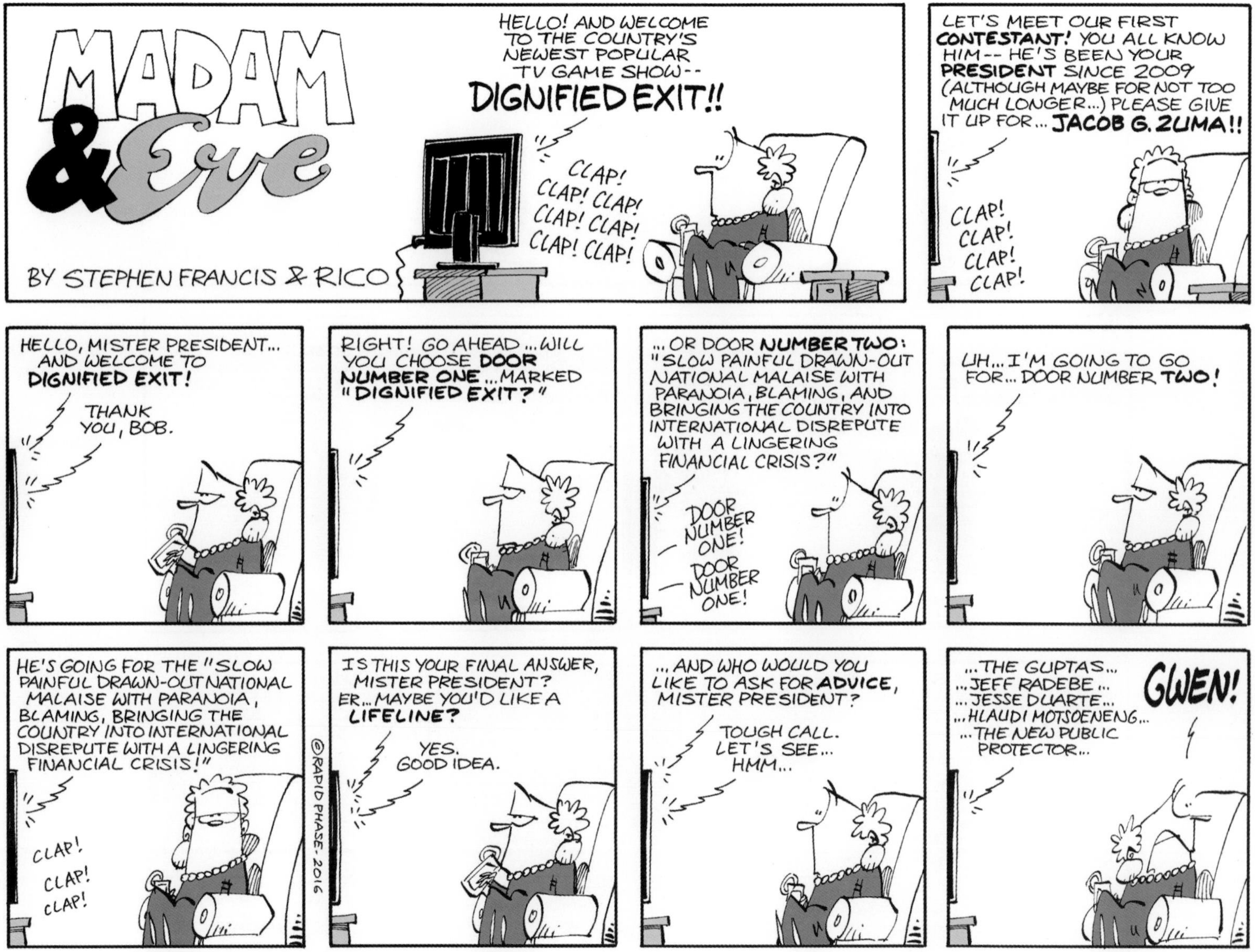
MADAM & Eve
BY STEPHEN FRANCIS & RICO
HELLO! AND WELCOME TO THE COUNTRY'S NEWEST POPULAR TV GAME SHOW--
DIGNIFIED EXIT!!
CLAP! CLAP! CLAP! CLAP! CLAP! CLAP! CLAP!
LET'S MEET OUR FIRST CONTESTANT! YOU ALL KNOW HIM-- HE'S BEEN YOUR PRESIDENT SINCE 2009 (ALTHOUGH MAYBE FOR NOT TOO MUCH LONGER...) PLEASE GIVE IT UP FOR... JACOB G. ZUMA!!
CLAP! CLAP! CLAP! CLAP!
HELLO, MISTER PRESIDENT... AND WELCOME TO DIGNIFIED EXIT!
THANK YOU, BOB.
RIGHT! GO AHEAD ...WILL YOU CHOOSE DOOR NUMBER ONE ...MARKED "DIGNIFIED EXIT?"
...OR DOOR NUMBER TWO: "SLOW PAINFUL DRAWN-OUT NATIONAL MALAISE WITH PARANOIA, BLAMING, AND BRINGING THE COUNTRY INTO INTERNATIONAL DISREPUTE WITH A LINGERING FINANCIAL CRISIS?"
DOOR NUMBER ONE!
DOOR NUMBER ONE!
UH... I'M GOING TO GO FOR... DOOR NUMBER TWO!
HE'S GOING FOR THE "SLOW PAINFUL DRAWN-OUT NATIONAL MALAISE WITH PARANOIA, BLAMING, BRINGING THE COUNTRY INTO INTERNATIONAL DISREPUTE WITH A LINGERING FINANCIAL CRISIS!"
CLAP! CLAP! CLAP!
IS THIS YOUR FINAL ANSWER, MISTER PRESIDENT? ER... MAYBE YOU'D LIKE A LIFELINE?
YES. GOOD IDEA.
© RAPID PHASE - 2016
...AND WHO WOULD YOU LIKE TO ASK FOR ADVICE, MISTER PRESIDENT?
TOUGH CALL. LET'S SEE... HMM...
...THE GUPTAS... ...JEFF RADEBE... ...JESSE DUARTE... ...HLAUDI MOTSOENENG... ...THE NEW PUBLIC PROTECTOR...
GWEN!

GASP!
N-NO!

IT CAN'T BE!
NOT **AGAIN**!!

QUICK, YOU FOOL!
THE SIGN! GET
THE **SIGN**!!

WHY DOES THIS ALWAYS
HAPPEN TO **ME**?!

MUST BE
COINCIDENCE.

SANTA
BACK
IN
30min

COMING UP...THE NEW
REVISED SABC
LOCAL PROGRAMME
SCHEDULE FOR THE
HOLIDAY SEASON...

FIRST UP...
"DESIGNATED BOARD
SURVIVOR"...
FOLLOWED BY...
"KEEPING UP WITH
THE GUPTAS"...

THEN...
"THE BIG BANG
HLAUDI THEORY"...
AND
"DAYS OF OUR
LIES."

FOLLOWED BY OUR
BRAND NEW
COMEDY DRAMA:
"HOUSE OF RACE
CARDS."
...ENJOY!

CONGRATULATIONS,
MOM -- NOBODY
DESERVES IT
MORE THAN YOU!

...AND WE COULDN'T
BE **PROUDER**.

Person *of the Year*
TIME

THANK YOU!
THANK YOU!
IT WAS
NOTHING!!

NO MORE
LEFTOVER
BEEF
CURRIES.

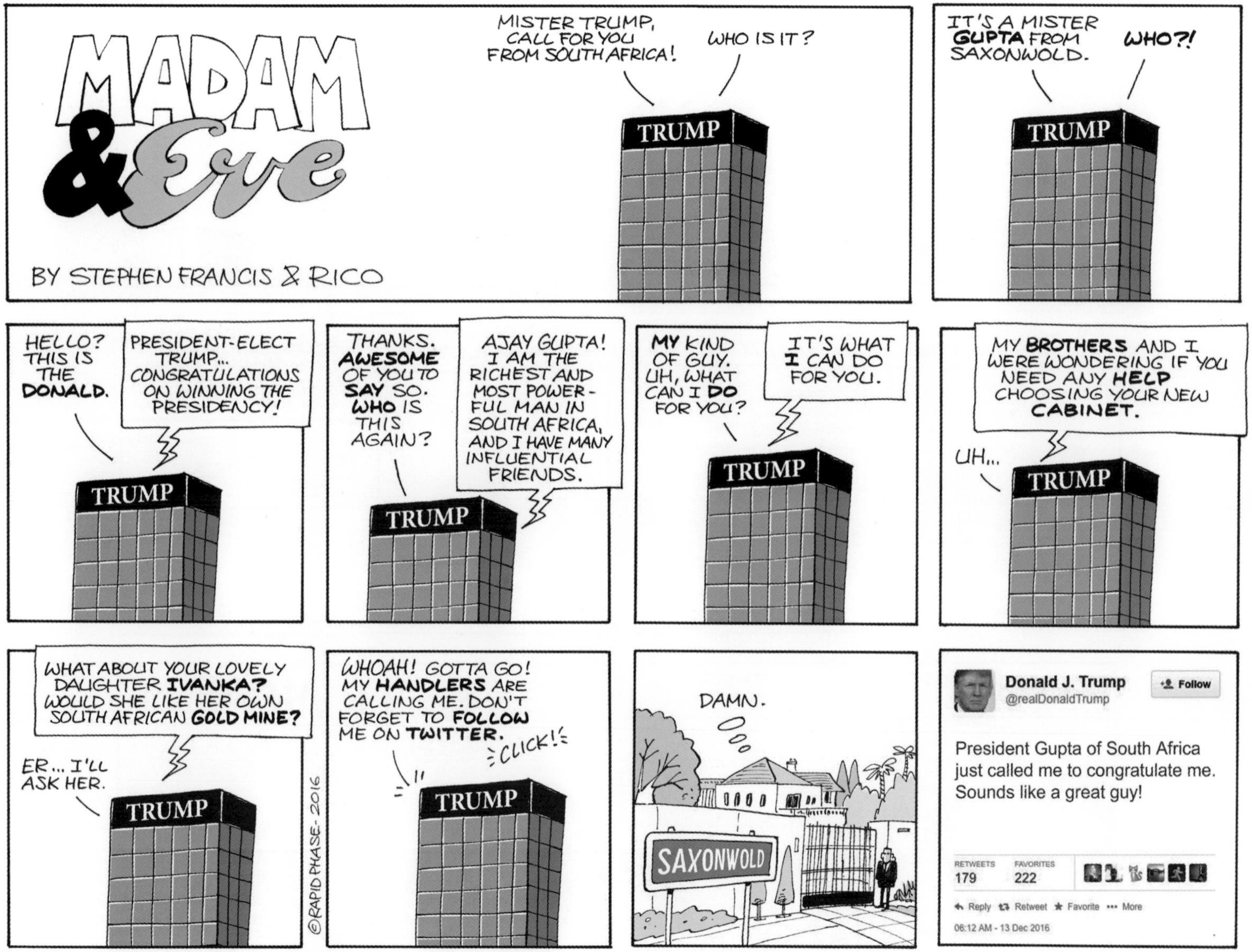
MADAM & Eve
BY STEPHEN FRANCIS & RICO
MISTER TRUMP, CALL FOR YOU FROM SOUTH AFRICA!
WHO IS IT?
TRUMP
IT'S A MISTER GUPTA FROM SAXONWOLD.
WHO?!
HELLO? THIS IS THE DONALD.
PRESIDENT-ELECT TRUMP... CONGRATULATIONS ON WINNING THE PRESIDENCY!
THANKS. AWESOME OF YOU TO SAY SO. WHO IS THIS AGAIN?
AJAY GUPTA! I AM THE RICHEST AND MOST POWER-FUL MAN IN SOUTH AFRICA, AND I HAVE MANY INFLUENTIAL FRIENDS.
MY KIND OF GUY. UH, WHAT CAN I DO FOR YOU?
IT'S WHAT I CAN DO FOR YOU.
MY BROTHERS AND I WERE WONDERING IF YOU NEED ANY HELP CHOOSING YOUR NEW CABINET.
UH...
WHAT ABOUT YOUR LOVELY DAUGHTER IVANKA? WOULD SHE LIKE HER OWN SOUTH AFRICAN GOLD MINE?
ER... I'LL ASK HER.
©RAPID PHASE-2016
WHOAH! GOTTA GO! MY HANDLERS ARE CALLING ME. DON'T FORGET TO FOLLOW ME ON TWITTER.
CLICK!
DAMN.
SAXONWOLD
Donald J. Trump
@realDonaldTrump
Follow
President Gupta of South Africa just called me to congratulate me. Sounds like a great guy!
RETWEETS 179
FAVORITES 222
Reply Retweet Favorite More
06:12 AM - 13 Dec 2016

FIRST OF ALL, I WANT TO APPLAUD PEOPLE WHO RECOGNISE THIS WONDERFUL PERSON CALLED FATHER CHRISTMAS!

FATHER CHRISTMAS IS FATHER CHRISTMAS! AND THERE IS ONLY ONE FATHER CHRISTMAS!

FROM NOW ON, ALL TOYS WILL BE MADE 90% LOCALLY AT THE NORTH POLE AND --

AAAH!! ...ANOTHER SABC NIGHTMARE.

TEN TV BOARD MEMBERS ALWAYS WANTING **MORE**.

SIX GREW A CONSCIENCE AND THEN THERE WERE **FOUR**.

FOUR TV BOARD MEMBERS GETTING LITTLE **DONE**.

PARLIAMENT CAME DOWN ON THEM... AND THEN THERE WAS **ONE**.

ONE TV BOARD MEMBER HAVING LITTLE **FUN**.

HE FINALLY SAW THE LIGHT AND **QUIT**... AND THEN THERE WERE **NONE**.

ONE **EX-CEO** ON A "CLOUDY" DAY THEY CAUGHT HIM IN (ALLEGED) **FRAUD**... AND TOOK HIM **AWAY**.

...AND THEN THERE (REALLY) WERE NONE.

AND SO... THE **THREE KINGS** ARRIVED WITH BEAUTIFUL PRESENTS.

THREE KINGS OFFERING **PRESENTS?!** WHAT WERE THEIR NAMES?

AJAY, ATUL AND RAJESH.

MOM! HO. HO. HO.

www.madamandeve.co.za

TOOT!!

HAPPY NEW YEAR!!

I WAS THINKING... WHEN DOES THE "NEW YEAR" ACTUALLY TURN "HAPPY?"

THE LAST DAY OF SCHOOL HOLIDAYS.

©RAPID PHASE · 2016   www.madamandeve.co.za

PUK. PUK. PUK.

COCK-A DOODLE DOO!!

HAPPY NEW YEAR! ACCORDING TO THE CHINESE CALENDAR, IT'S THE YEAR OF THE ROOSTER!

PUK.

©RAPID PHASE · 2017   www.madamandeve.co.za

SLAM!!

WELL, YOU REALLY COCKED THAT ONE UP.

HISTORY MAY RECORD IT DIFFERENTLY.

PUK. PUK. PUK.

HAPPY NEW YEAR, MISTER PRESIDENT!

THANK YOU. AND...

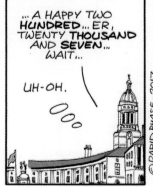

...A HAPPY TWO HUNDRED... ER, TWENTY THOUSAND AND SEVEN... WAIT...

UH-OH.

©RAPID PHASE · 2017   www.madamandeve.co.za

...ONE PLUS SIXTEEN EQUALS...?

COME ON, YOU CAN DO IT.

HAPPY TWO DOUBLE-ZERO ONE-SEVEN TO YOU!

CLOSE ENOUGH.

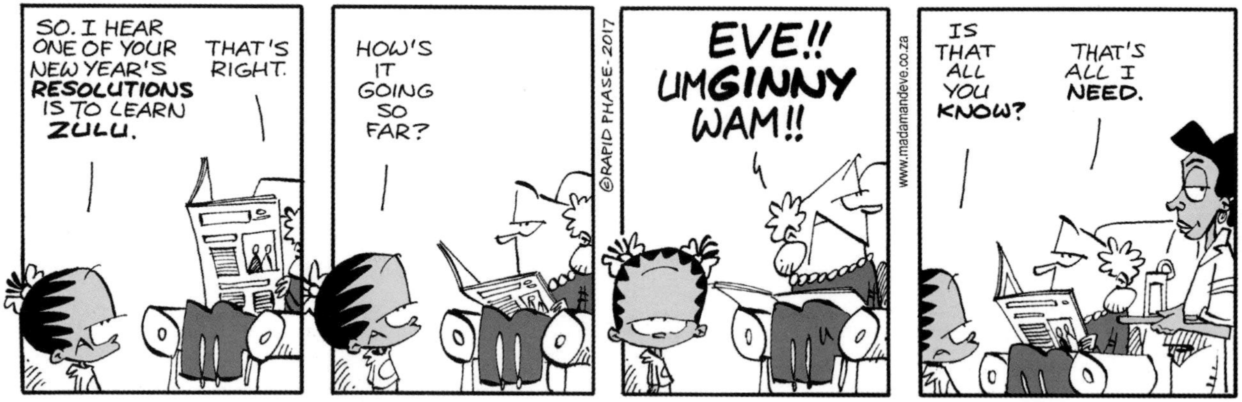

SO. I HEAR ONE OF YOUR NEW YEAR'S **RESOLUTIONS** IS TO LEARN **ZULU.**
THAT'S RIGHT.
HOW'S IT GOING SO FAR?
©RAPID PHASE-2017
EVE!! UMGINNY WAM!!
www.madamandeve.co.za
IS THAT ALL YOU **KNOW?**
THAT'S ALL I **NEED.**

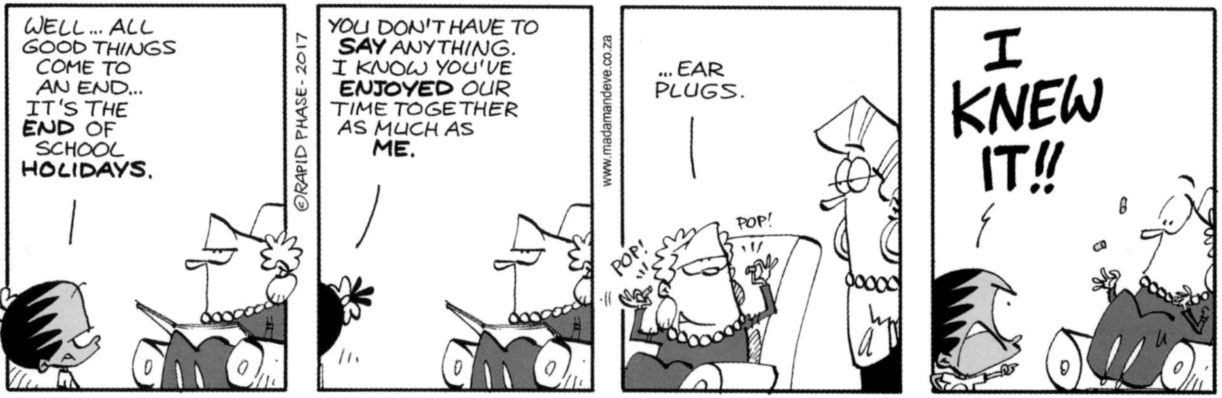

WELL... ALL GOOD THINGS COME TO AN END... IT'S THE **END** OF SCHOOL **HOLIDAYS.**
©RAPID PHASE-2017
YOU DON'T HAVE TO **SAY** ANYTHING. I KNOW YOU'VE **ENJOYED** OUR TIME TOGETHER AS MUCH AS **ME.**
www.madamandeve.co.za
...EAR PLUGS.
POP!
POP!
I KNEW IT!!

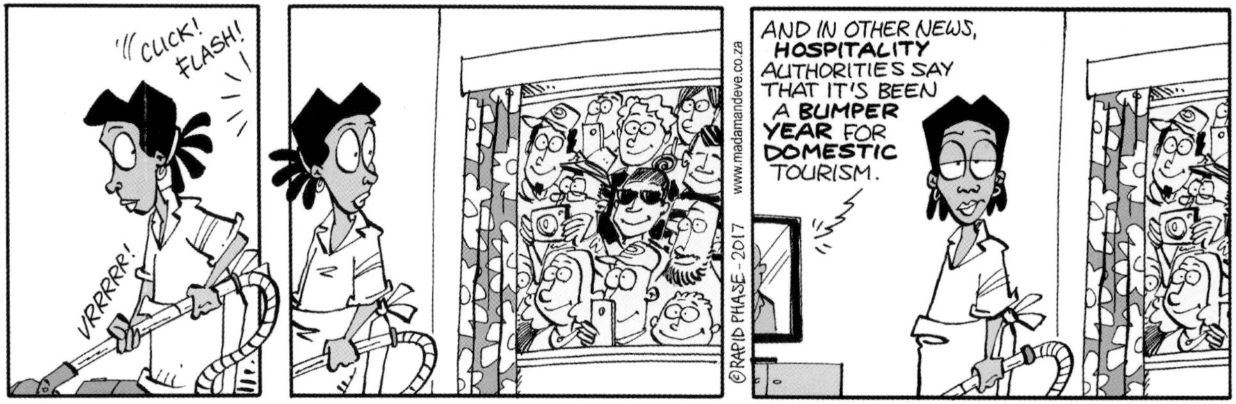

CLICK!
FLASH!
VRRRRR!
www.madamandeve.co.za
©RAPID PHASE-2017
AND IN OTHER NEWS, **HOSPITALITY** AUTHORITIES SAY THAT IT'S BEEN A **BUMPER YEAR** FOR **DOMESTIC** TOURISM.

MADAM & Eve

BY STEPHEN FRANCIS & RICO

HELLO! MY NAME IS **EVE SISULU**, AND I'LL BE YOUR DOMESTIC MAINTENANCE ADVISOR FOR TODAY.

BEFORE WE FLY OFF INTO **2017**... THERE ARE A FEW **SAFETY** RULES AND REGULATIONS... SO PLEASE PAY **ATTENTION**.

THIS IS A "NO SMOKING" HOUSE... SO **NO SMOKING**, UNLESS... IT'S COMING FROM MY **IRONING BOARD**, IN WHICH CASE... OOPS.

THE **EXITS** ARE HERE... HERE... AND HERE. ALTHOUGH, IN THE EVENT OF AN **EMERGENCY**, THEY'LL BE LOCKED, BOLTED AND BARRED. SO, GOOD LUCK.

IN CASE OF **NAUSEA** OR VOMITING, DUE TO **NEWS HEADLINES** OR **STATE CAPTURE**, SICKNESS BAGS HAVE BEEN PLACED UNDER YOUR SEAT.

AT SOME POINT DURING THE YEAR, YOUR DOMESTIC WORKER WILL ASK FOR **LEAVE** OR A **WAGE INCREASE**. FEEL FREE TO OFFER YOUR **USUAL** EXCUSES.

IN THE LIKELY EVENT OF **GOVERNMENT CORRUPTION**, OXYGEN MASKS WILL **DROP** FROM THE **CEILING**.

... YOU WILL, HOWEVER, NEED TO PAY AN **OXYGEN LICENCE** TO HLAUDI MOTSOENENG.

©RAPID PHASE – 2017

IF YOU WISH TO PURCHASE DISCOUNT **DUTY FREE** GIFTS, GIVE ME YOUR MONEY... MY COUSIN WORKS IN THE AIRPORT **BAGGAGE** DEPARTMENT.

IN JUST A MOMENT... AN ATTENDANT WILL PASS BY WITH A **DRINKS TROLLEY**... SO ENJOY THE START OF THE YEAR! THANK YOU!

YAY!

I THOUGHT SHE DID THAT RATHER **WELL**.

DOUBLE GIN & TONIC. LOTS OF ICE!

SQUEAK SQUEAK

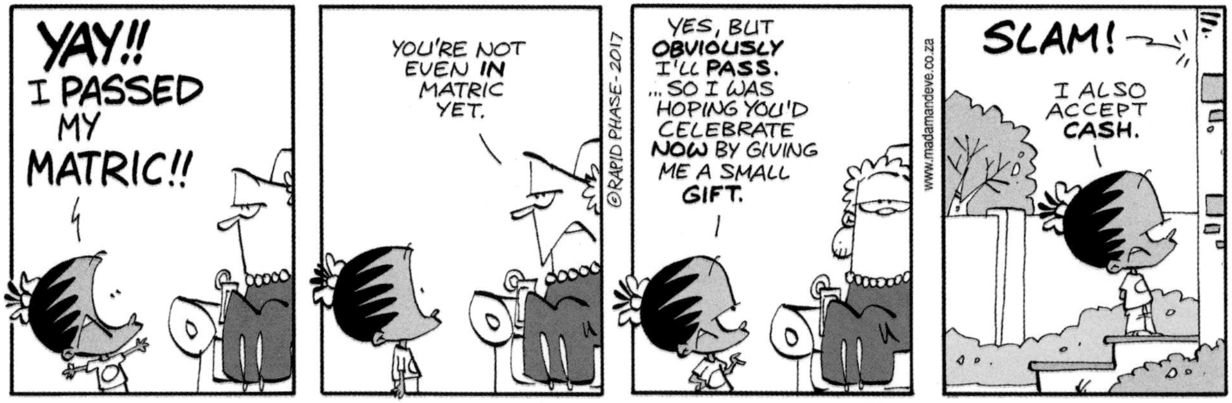
YAY!! I PASSED MY MATRIC!!
YOU'RE NOT EVEN IN MATRIC YET.
©RAPID PHASE-2017
YES, BUT OBVIOUSLY I'LL PASS. ...SO I WAS HOPING YOU'D CELEBRATE NOW BY GIVING ME A SMALL GIFT.
www.madamandeve.co.za
SLAM!
I ALSO ACCEPT CASH.

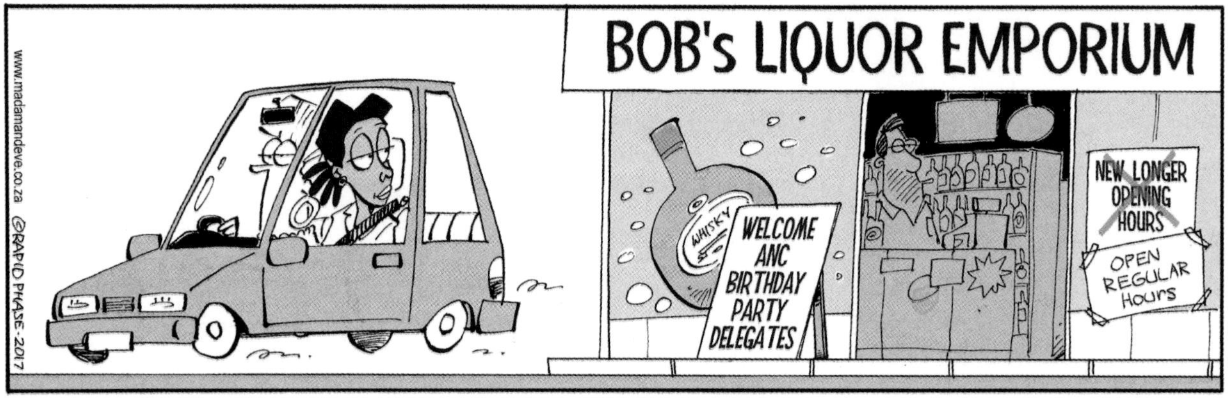
www.madamandeve.co.za ©RAPID PHASE-2017
BOB's LIQUOR EMPORIUM
WHISKY
WELCOME ANC BIRTHDAY PARTY DELEGATES
NEW LONGER OPENING HOURS
OPEN REGULAR Hours

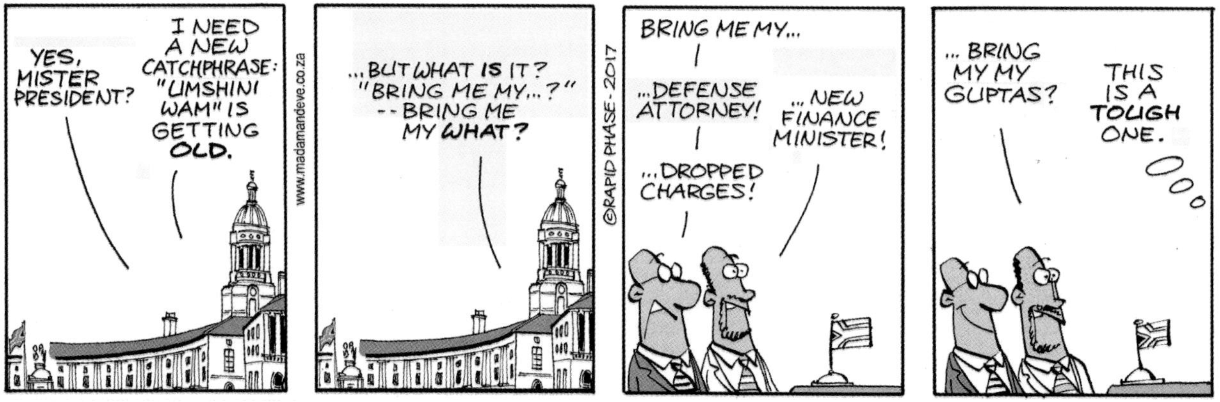
YES, MISTER PRESIDENT?
I NEED A NEW CATCHPHRASE: "UMSHINI WAM" IS GETTING OLD.
www.madamandeve.co.za
...BUT WHAT IS IT? "BRING ME MY...?" --BRING ME MY WHAT?
©RAPID PHASE-2017
BRING ME MY...
...DEFENSE ATTORNEY!
...DROPPED CHARGES!
...NEW FINANCE MINISTER!
...BRING MY MY GUPTAS?
THIS IS A TOUGH ONE.

MADAM & Eve

BY STEPHEN FRANCIS & RICO

LET'S SEE IF THIS MAGIC LAMP STILL WORKS.

UMGENIE WAM!!

RUB! RUB!

YES, MASTER! WHAT DO YOU COMMAND?

POOF!

YOU KNOW, YOU LOOK A LOT LIKE ATUL GUPTA.

I KNOW. I GET THAT ALL THE TIME. WHAT ARE YOUR THREE WISHES?

LET'S SEE... I WANT TO BE PRESIDENT FOR LIFE... I WANT ALL CORRUPTION CHARGES DROPPED.

... AND I WANT DES VAN ROOYEN TO BE FINANCE MINISTER AGAIN!

SIGH THERE ARE SOME THINGS EVEN A GENIE CAN'T DO!

RIGHT. CAN WE TALK ABOUT MY WISHES NOW?

YOUR WISHES?

YOU'RE A GENIE! WHAT COULD YOU POSSIBLY WANT?!

GRAPID PHASE · 2017

... CAPTURE WHAT?!

LET HIM SLEEP. BETTER HERE THAN IN PARLIAMENT.

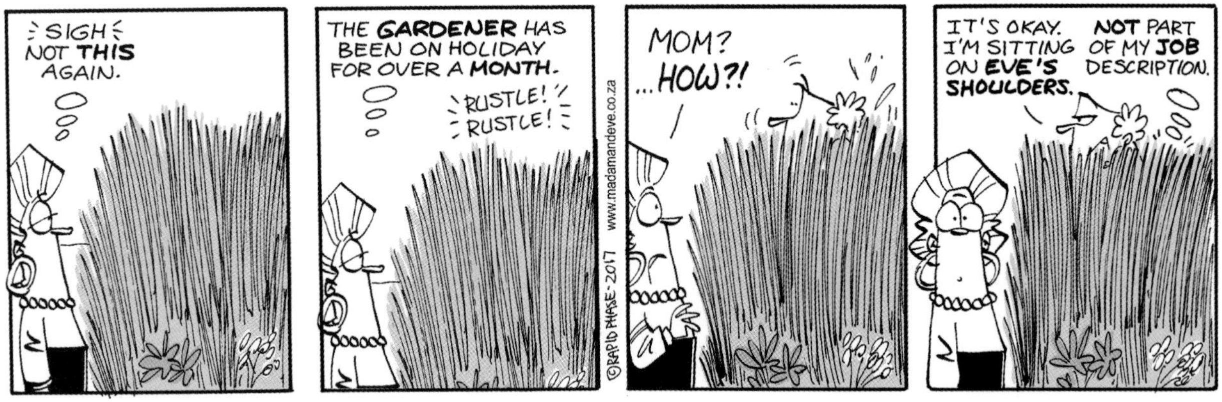
SIGH
NOT THIS AGAIN.
THE GARDENER HAS BEEN ON HOLIDAY FOR OVER A MONTH.
RUSTLE! RUSTLE!
©RAPID PHASE-2017 www.madamandeve.co.za
MOM? ...HOW?!
IT'S OKAY. I'M SITTING ON EVE'S SHOULDERS.
NOT PART OF MY JOB DESCRIPTION.

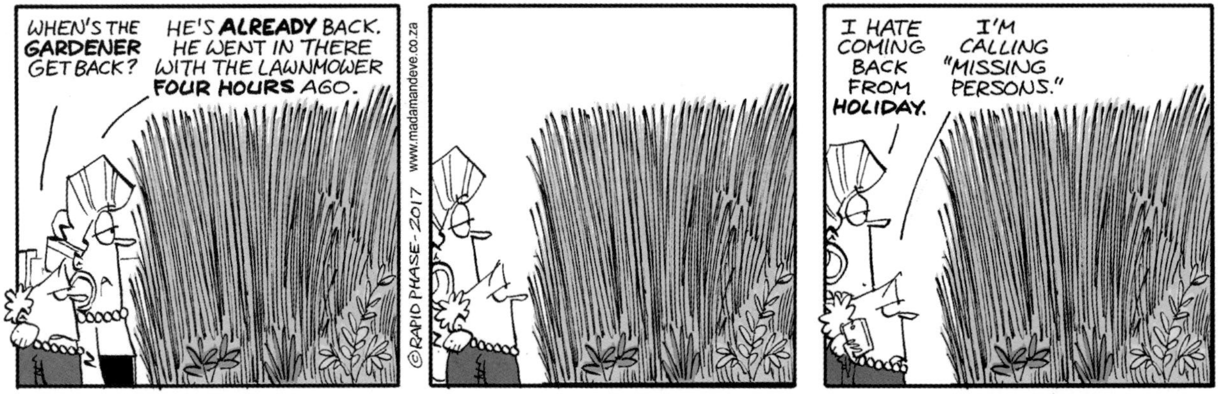
WHEN'S THE GARDENER GET BACK?
HE'S ALREADY BACK. HE WENT IN THERE WITH THE LAWNMOWER FOUR HOURS AGO.
©RAPID PHASE-2017 www.madamandeve.co.za
I HATE COMING BACK FROM HOLIDAY.
I'M CALLING "MISSING PERSONS."

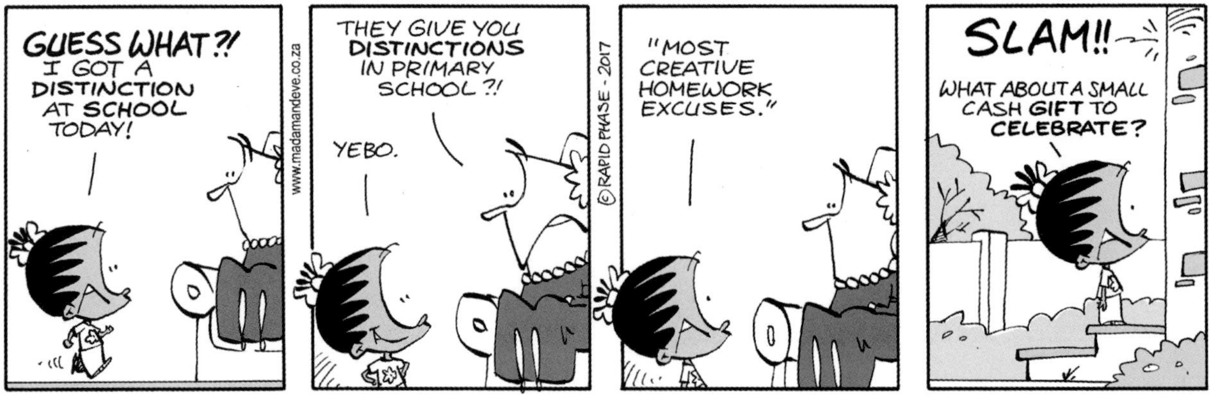
GUESS WHAT?! I GOT A DISTINCTION AT SCHOOL TODAY!
www.madamandeve.co.za
THEY GIVE YOU DISTINCTIONS IN PRIMARY SCHOOL?!
YEBO.
©RAPID PHASE-2017
"MOST CREATIVE HOMEWORK EXCUSES."
SLAM!!
WHAT ABOUT A SMALL CASH GIFT TO CELEBRATE?

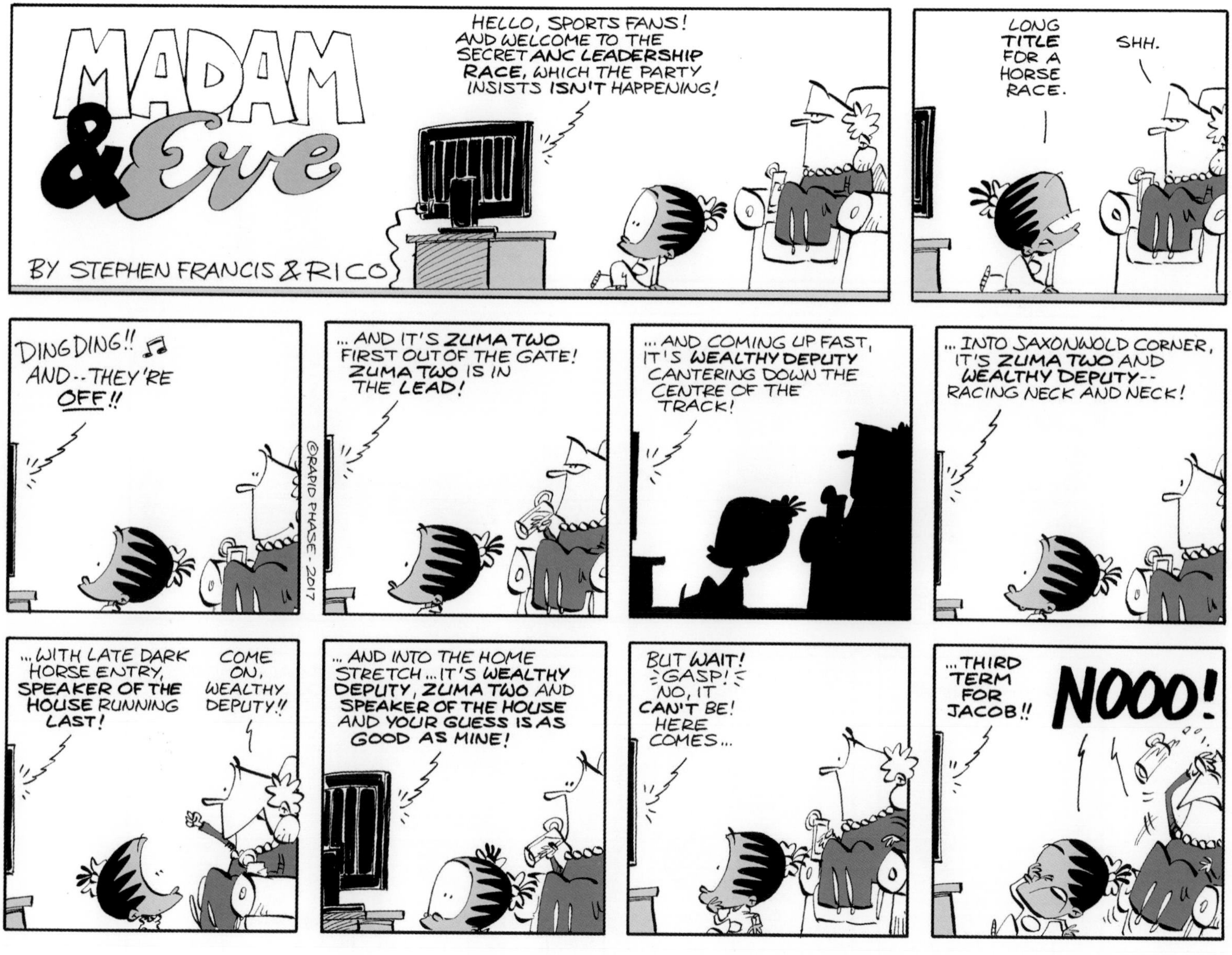
MADAM & Eve
BY STEPHEN FRANCIS & RICO
HELLO, SPORTS FANS! AND WELCOME TO THE SECRET ANC LEADERSHIP RACE, WHICH THE PARTY INSISTS ISN'T HAPPENING!
LONG TITLE FOR A HORSE RACE.
SHH.
DING DING!! AND--THEY'RE OFF!!
©RAPID PHASE-2017
...AND IT'S ZUMA TWO FIRST OUT OF THE GATE! ZUMA TWO IS IN THE LEAD!
...AND COMING UP FAST, IT'S WEALTHY DEPUTY CANTERING DOWN THE CENTRE OF THE TRACK!
...INTO SAXONWOLD CORNER, IT'S ZUMA TWO AND WEALTHY DEPUTY--RACING NECK AND NECK!
...WITH LATE DARK HORSE ENTRY, SPEAKER OF THE HOUSE RUNNING LAST!
COME ON, WEALTHY DEPUTY!!
...AND INTO THE HOME STRETCH...IT'S WEALTHY DEPUTY, ZUMA TWO AND SPEAKER OF THE HOUSE AND YOUR GUESS IS AS GOOD AS MINE!
BUT WAIT! GASP! NO, IT CAN'T BE! HERE COMES...
...THIRD TERM FOR JACOB!!
NOOO!

MADAM & EVE'S KNOW YOUR FIRES

VEGETATION FIRE

CAPE TOWN

AUTOMOBILE FIRE

KUGA

PANTS ON FIRE

TRUMP

KUGA NATIONAL PARK

KUGA

"ENGLISH GRAMMAR QUIZ..."

"QUESTION #1: WHAT'S THE DIFFERENCE BETWEEN **REDEPLOY** AND **RECALL**?"

"**REDEPLOY**...MEANS YOU END UP AS A GOVERNMENT AMBASSADOR SOMEWHERE."

"**RECALL**...MEANS YOU END UP BACK AT THE **FORD** FACTORY."

MADAM & Eve

BY STEPHEN FRANCIS & RICO

SLAM!

HOW WAS SCHOOL TODAY?

UNBELIEVABLE! IT'S UNBELIEVABLE HOW GOOD I AM AT GOING TO SCHOOL!

YEBO. NOBODY IS BETTER AT SCHOOL THAN ME!

I THOUGHT YOU WERE HAVING **PROBLEMS** WITH YOUR TEACHER?

THAT'S **FAKE** NEWS! I **LOVE** MY TEACHER! **NOBODY** LOVES THE TEACHER MORE THAN ME!

I'M 100% **BEHIND** MY TEACHER! I **TOTALLY** HAVE MY TEACHER'S BACK! I'M THE **BEST** AT HAVING MY TEACHER'S BACK! THE **BEST**!

I'M STARTING TO WORRY THAT THIS "**TRUMP**" INFLUENCE IS BECOMING A GLOBAL PHENOMENON.

IT'S THE AGE OF **ALTERNATIVE FACTS**! ANYONE CAN BE A PRESIDENT! **NO EXPERIENCE NECESSARY**!

© RAPID PHASE · 2017

THAT'S WHY... WHEN I GROW UP, I'M GOING INTO POLITICS!

SIGH.

NOW WHAT ARE YOU DOING?

GETTING MY KELLYANNE CONWAY ON.

EVE!! WHERE'S MY GIN & TONIC?!

COUNCILMAN VUSI! THE CORRUPTION INVESTIGATORS ARE HERE!

LET THEM COME! WHAT DO I HAVE TO HIDE?

UH... ACTUALLY LOTS, SIR.

THIS WHOLE THING IS AN ASSAULT ON MY... MY...

...WHAT DO YOU CALL THAT THING ALL POLITICIANS ARE SUPPOSED TO HAVE?

"INTEGRITY," SIR?

SIRI! ...DEFINE "INTEGRITY."

DONALD TRUMP: THE FORMATIVE YEARS

THIS IS GOING TO BE THE BEST HOMEWORK EVER. BELIEVE ME. I DO GREAT HOMEWORK. THE BEST. I'LL SUBMIT MY HOMEWORK RIGHT AFTER I'M ELECTED CLASS PRESIDENT.

THANDI -- WHY DON'T YOU JUST TELL THE TRUTH? THAT YOU DIDN'T DO YOUR HOMEWORK AND HAVE NO INTENTION OF DOING HOMEWORK!

FIRST OF ALL, THAT'S AN ALTERNATIVE FACT.

AND FRANKLY, THAT'S NOT THE NARRATIVE I'D LIKE TO GO WITH TODAY.

..."NARRATIVE"?

WATCH CNN.

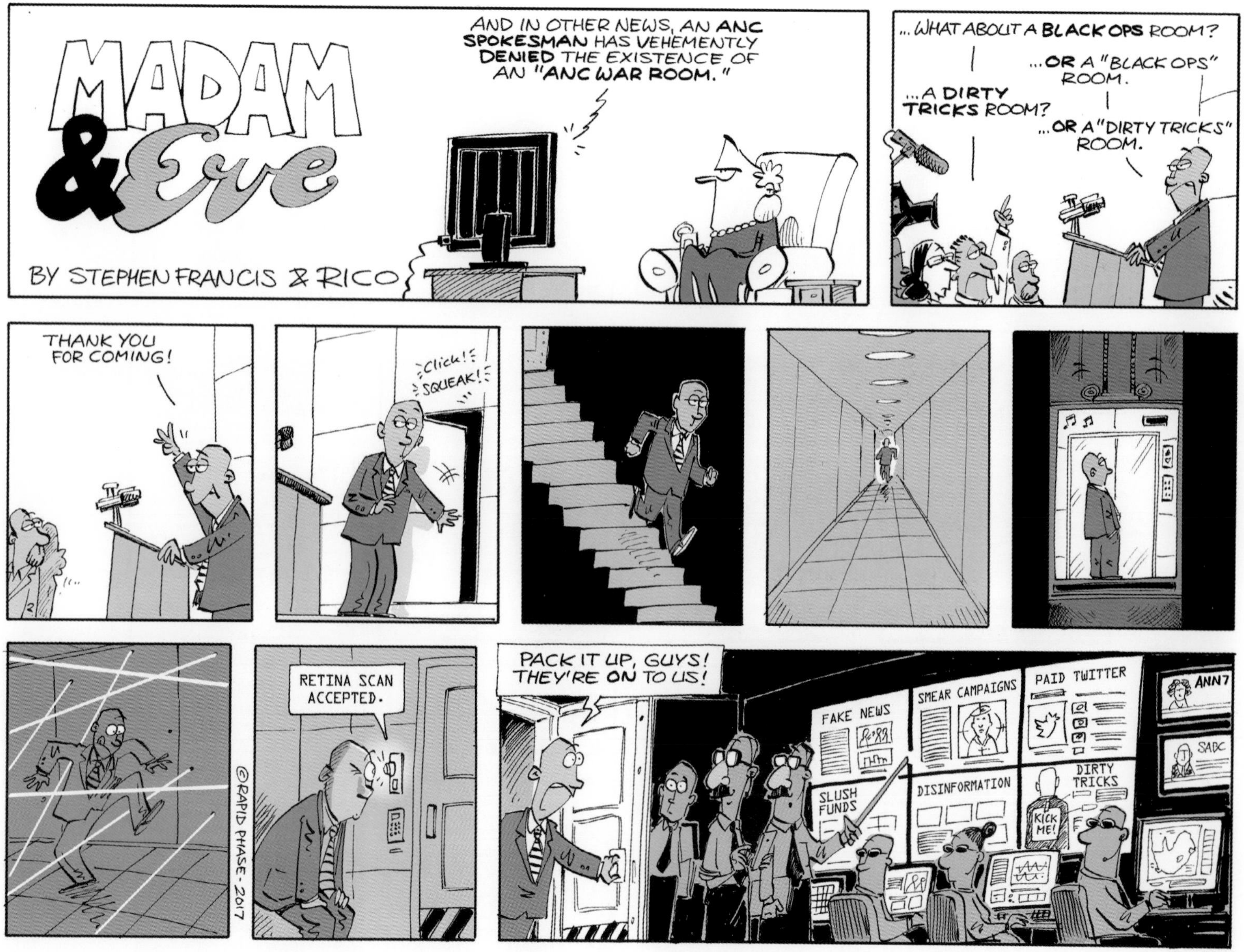
MADAM & Eve
BY STEPHEN FRANCIS & RICO
AND IN OTHER NEWS, AN ANC SPOKESMAN HAS VEHEMENTLY DENIED THE EXISTENCE OF AN "ANC WAR ROOM."
...WHAT ABOUT A BLACK OPS ROOM?
...OR A "BLACK OPS" ROOM.
...A DIRTY TRICKS ROOM?
...OR A "DIRTY TRICKS" ROOM.
THANK YOU FOR COMING!
Click!
SQUEAK!
RETINA SCAN ACCEPTED.
©RAPID PHASE-2017
PACK IT UP, GUYS! THEY'RE ON TO US!
FAKE NEWS
SMEAR CAMPAIGNS
PAID TWITTER
ANN7
SABC
SLUSH FUNDS
DISINFORMATION
DIRTY TRICKS
KICK ME!

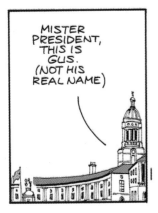

MISTER PRESIDENT, THIS IS GUS. (NOT HIS REAL NAME)

HE'LL BE HEADING OUR NEW TOP SECRET ANC ELECTION "BLACK OPS" AND "DIRTY TRICKS" DEPARTMENT.

VERY GOOD. AND BY THE WAY... I LOVE YOUR DISGUISE.

WHAT DISGUISE?

YES, MISTER PRESIDENT?

YES. I UNDERSTAND AMERICANS CALL DONALD TRUMP POTUS.

UH, THAT'S RIGHT, SIR.

I WAS WONDERING. WHAT DO SOUTH AFRICANS CALL ME?

WHOAH! WILL YOU LOOK AT THE TIME!

DON'T YOU HAVE A CABINET MEETING, SIR?

UP NEXT. FAKE NEWS.

FOLLOWED BY EYEWITNESS FAKE NEWS...

...ON SOUTH AFRICA'S FIRST ALTERNATIVE FACT STATION.

WHAT CHANNEL IS THAT?

ANN 7.

MADAM & Eve

BY STEPHEN FRANCIS & RICO

THE MESOZOIC ERA: ONE MILLION YEARS BC! (BEFORE CLINTON)

TROPICAL HEAT. BUZZING INSECTS. WHEN **SUDDENLY**...

...A GIANT FOOT DRAINS THE SWAMP!

TRUMP!

THE GROUND **SHAKES** WITH HIS **UNBELIEVABLE** AWESOMENESS!

TRUMP!!

UMP! MP!

TRU TRU

IT'S THE **TRUMPASAURUS WRECKS!**

SELF-PROCLAIMED KING OF THE DINOSAURS.

EASY TO **SPOT** WITH ITS TINY **HANDS** AND **YELLOW PLUMAGE!**

...ANY QUESTIONS SO FAR?

© RAPID PHASE - 2017

IS THE TRUMPA-SAURUS ARMOUR-PLATED?

...ACTUALLY, IT'S INCREDIBLY **THIN-SKINNED!**

I BET HE HAS A MIGHTY ROAR!

UH... IT'S MORE OF AN EMBARASSING TWITTER, ACTUALLY.

I CAN'T **BELIEVE** IT! MY TEACHER GAVE ME AN A+ ON MY **TRUMPASAURUS** REPORT!

"TRUMPASAURUS?" WHERE DID YOU DO YOUR **RESEARCH?**

CNN.

THUMPA!
THUMPA!
THUMPA!
THUMPA!

EVERY NIGHT THE SAME THING FROM OUR NEIGHBOURS! PARTIES AND LOUD MUSIC!

THUMPA!
THUMPA!
THUMPA!
THUMPA!

THAT'S ODD. IT JUST STOPPED.

FINALLY!

TODAY'S TOP STORY: **CORRUPTION INVESTIGATORS** HAVE CONFISCATED A **R 80 000 SOUND SYSTEM** FROM ACTING POLICE COMMISSIONER PHAHLANE'S HOUSE.

ALTERNATIVE FACTS

FIRE POOL

ALTERNATIVE PROMISES

A BETTER LIFE FOR ALL
VOTE ANC

ALTERNATIVE GOVERNMENT

SAXONWOLD

ALTERNATIVE REALITY

SABC

ALTERNATIVE WAGE INCREASE

ALTERNATIVE PROFITS

SOUTH AFRICAN

ALTERNATIVE DEMOCRACY

PARLIAMENT
SANDF SANDF SANDF

ALTERNATIVE PRESIDENT
HEH. HEH. HEH.

© RAPID PHASE - 2017
www.madamandeve.co.za

62

MADAM & EVE

BY STEPHEN FRANCIS & RICO

ALL OF SOUTH AFRICA LOVED SANTA & ELVES.

BUT THE GRINCHES SOUGHT CHRISTMAS...

HEH. HEH. HEH.

...ALL FOR THEMSELVES!

SO THEY PLOTTED IN SAXONWOLD (THEY OWNED THE WHOLE STREET)

WE'LL INVITE FATHER CHRISTMAS FOR A TOP SECRET MEET.

SAXONWOLD

THE NORTH POLE SOUNDS WONDERFUL! CAN WE BUY OUR WAY IN?!

WHAT DO YOU WANT FOR A DEAL THAT'S A WIN-WIN?

MONEY? A GOLD MINE? WE'LL FIND SOMETHING YET!

A REINDEER RESHUFFLE? ...YOUR OWN PRIVATE JET?

FATHER CHRISTMAS WAS OUTRAGED!

YOU THINK I'M CORRUPT?!

HE ROSE FROM THE TABLE (LIKE, VERY ABRUPT.)

THE GRINCHES WERE GOBSMACKED! THEY GAVE IT THEIR ALL!

TIC TIC TIC TIC

SANTA TWEETED A HASHTAG: #ALLGRINCHESMUSTFALL

WAIT A MINUTE! STOP THE STORY! THIS IS ALL JUST-- --ALLEGORY.

©RAPID PHASE—2016

THEN WHY DON'T WE END ON A NOTE OF GOOD CHEER?

...AND WISH PEACE ON EARTH TO EVERYONE HERE!

...AND THEY HEARD HIM EXCLAIM AS HE DROVE OUT OF SIGHT...

MERRY CHRISTMAS, SOUTH AFRICA... AND TO ALL A GOOD NIGHT!

MADAM & EVE's CHRISTMAS HOLIDAY TIPS #2

HOUSE OWNERS: IF YOU GO AWAY FOR AN EXTENDED HOLIDAY, BE SURE TO CANCEL ALL NEWSPAPER AND MAGAZINE SUBSCRIPTIONS!

OTHERWISE, *BURGLARS* MIGHT TAKE ADVANTAGE OF YOU!

MADAM & EVE's CHRISTMAS HOLIDAY TIPS #3

CHRISTMAS FRUITCAKES THAT HAVE BEEN *REGIFTED* FOR MANY YEARS MAKE EXCELLENT *DOORSTOPS* OR *PAPERWEIGHTS.*

MADAM & EVE's
CHRISTMAS HOLIDAY TIPS #4

BEFORE VISITING ONE OF FATHER CHRISTMAS'S *"HELPERS"*... MAKE SURE THEY REALLY *ARE* A FATHER CHRISTMAS *"HELPER."*

SANTA'S GROTTO

HO! HO! HO!

HO! HO! HO!

HO! HO! HO!

BOO HOO HOO!!

CREDIT CARD STATEMENT

BILLS

A few weeks ago in a *Galaxy* not so far, far away...

SAMSUNG

GET OUT OF HERE! IT'S GOING TO *EXPLODE!*

65

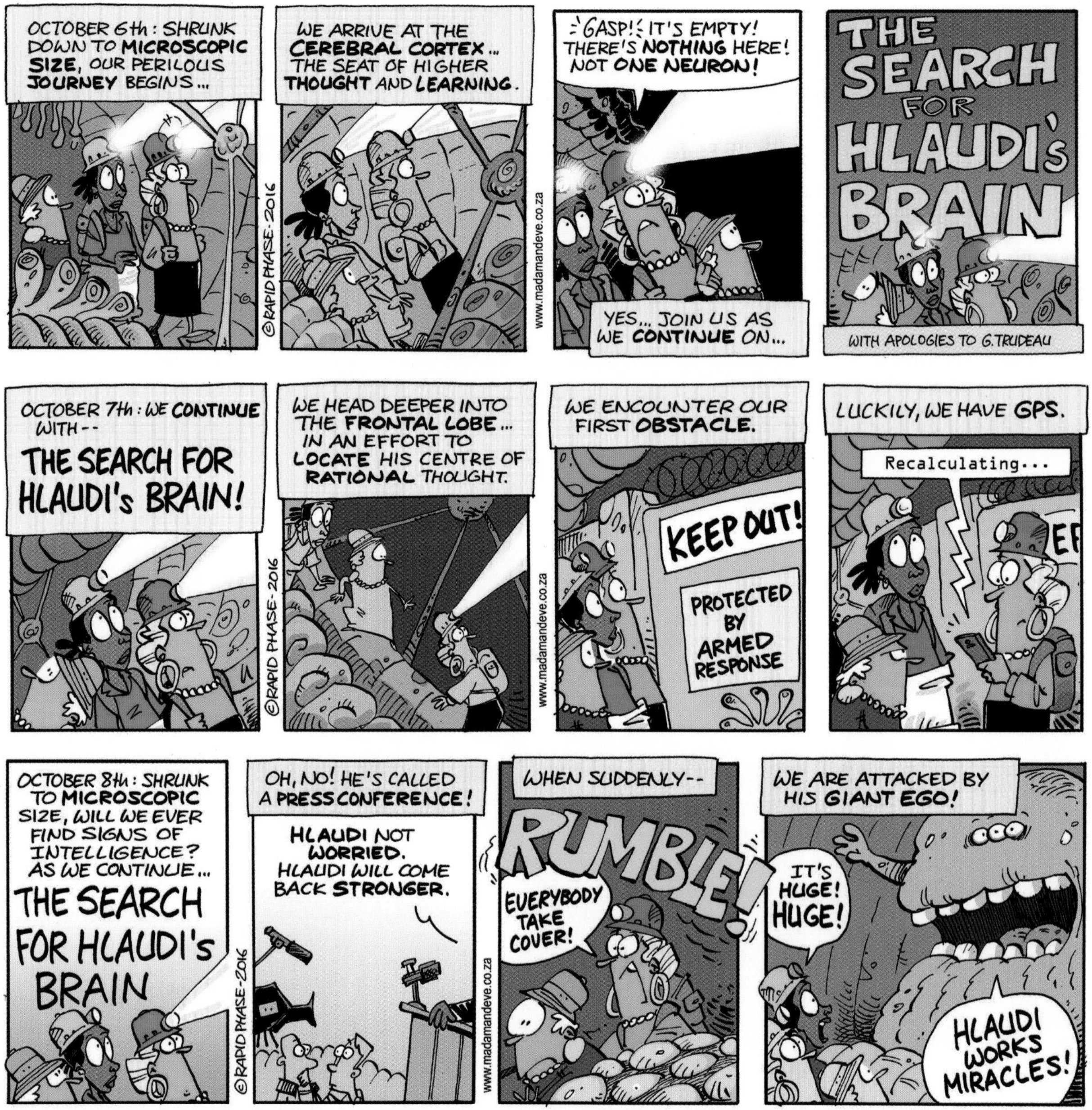
OCTOBER 6th: SHRUNK DOWN TO MICROSCOPIC SIZE, OUR PERILOUS JOURNEY BEGINS...
©RAPID PHASE-2016
WE ARRIVE AT THE CEREBRAL CORTEX... THE SEAT OF HIGHER THOUGHT AND LEARNING.
www.madamandeve.co.za
GASP! IT'S EMPTY! THERE'S NOTHING HERE! NOT ONE NEURON!
YES... JOIN US AS WE CONTINUE ON...
THE SEARCH FOR HLAUDI's BRAIN
WITH APOLOGIES TO G.TRUDEAU
OCTOBER 7th: WE CONTINUE WITH--
THE SEARCH FOR HLAUDI's BRAIN!
©RAPID PHASE-2016
WE HEAD DEEPER INTO THE FRONTAL LOBE... IN AN EFFORT TO LOCATE HIS CENTRE OF RATIONAL THOUGHT.
www.madamandeve.co.za
WE ENCOUNTER OUR FIRST OBSTACLE.
KEEP OUT!
PROTECTED BY ARMED RESPONSE
LUCKILY, WE HAVE GPS.
Recalculating...
OCTOBER 8th: SHRUNK TO MICROSCOPIC SIZE, WILL WE EVER FIND SIGNS OF INTELLIGENCE? AS WE CONTINUE...
THE SEARCH FOR HLAUDI's BRAIN
©RAPID PHASE-2016
OH, NO! HE'S CALLED A PRESS CONFERENCE!
HLAUDI NOT WORRIED. HLAUDI WILL COME BACK STRONGER.
www.madamandeve.co.za
WHEN SUDDENLY--
RUMBLE!
EVERYBODY TAKE COVER!
WE ARE ATTACKED BY HIS GIANT EGO!
IT'S HUGE! HUGE!
HLAUDI WORKS MIRACLES!

OUR HOPE IS SINKING FAST. WILL WE EVER WHAT WE'RE **LOOKING FOR**...

THE SEARCH FOR HLAUDI'S BRAIN!

OCTOBER 10th: WE CROSS A **SEA** OF INSECURITY.

WE SPY **NEURONS** AND BRAIN CELLS... NEVER **USED** OR **ATROPHIED**.

HOW CAN SOMEONE WITH SUCH **DIMINISHED** CRANIAL CAPACITY CONTINUE TO HOLD A SENIOR MANAGEMENT POST AT THE PUBLIC BROADCASTER.

THEN...

... WE GET OUR ANSWER. GRAFFITI ON THE CEREBELLUM WALL.

I KNEW IT!!

J ZUMA WUZ here!

AND... IN OTHER NEWS, **PRESIDENT ZUMA** HAS SAID HE PLANS TO WRITE A "TELL ALL" BOOK REVEALING THE WHOLE **TRUTH** WHEN HE **RETIRES**.

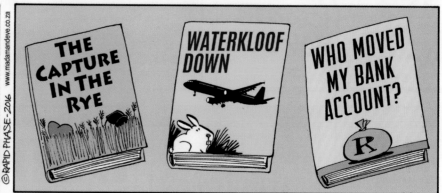

THE CAPTURE IN THE RYE

WATERKLOOF DOWN

WHO MOVED MY BANK ACCOUNT?

-VUSI'S RENT-A-GUARD-

MADAM & Eve

NEW SOUTH AFRICAN HORROR MOVIES

BY STEPHEN FRANCIS & RICO

TEXAS CHAINSAW CABINET MASSACRE

CREATURE FROM THE WHITE COLONIAL LAGOON

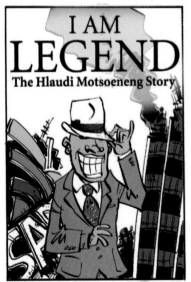

I AM LEGEND
The Hlaudi Motsoeneng Story

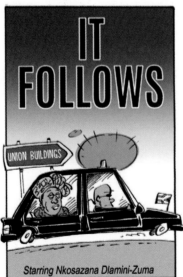

IT FOLLOWS

Starring Nkosazana Dlamini-Zuma

DAS BOOD

I KNOW WHAT YOU DID LAST SUMMER

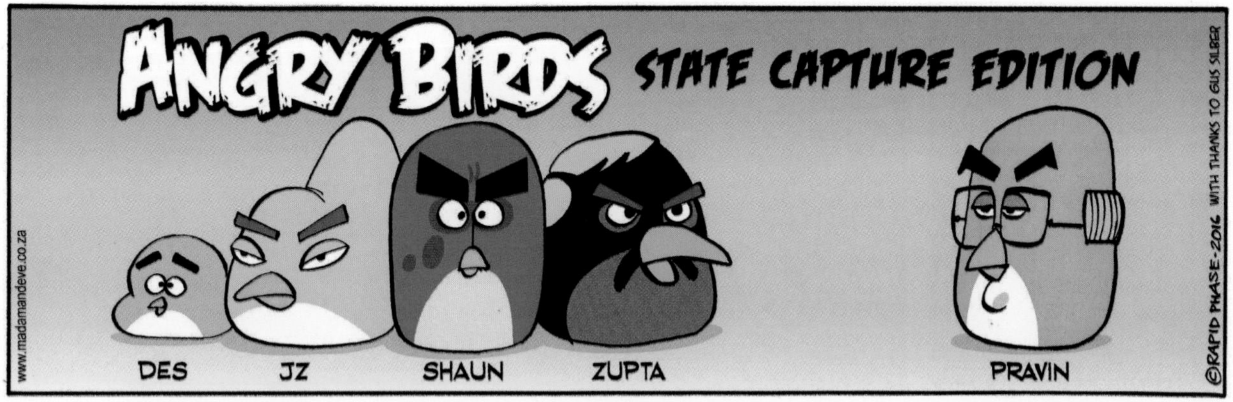
ANGRY BIRDS STATE CAPTURE EDITION
DES
JZ
SHAUN
ZUPTA
PRAVIN
www.madamandeve.co.za
©RAPID PHASE-2016 WITH THANKS TO GUS SILBER

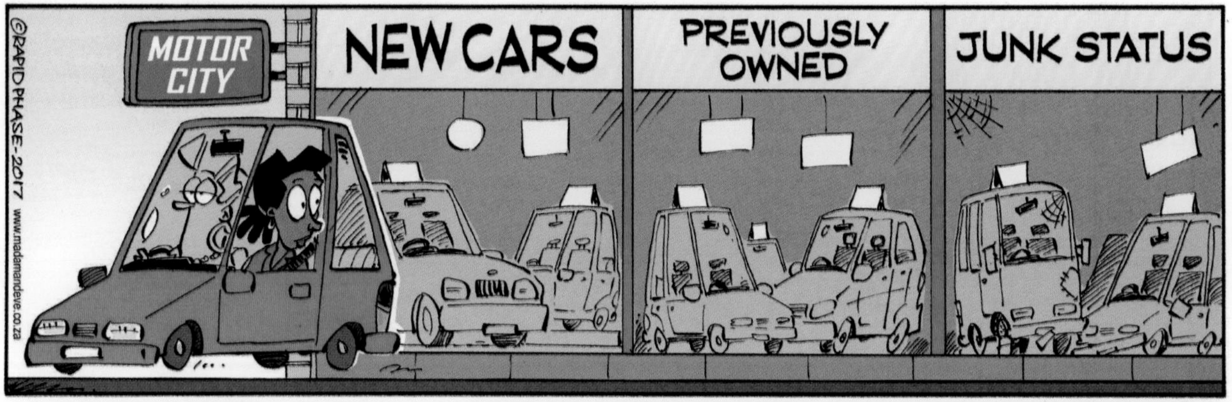
MOTOR CITY
NEW CARS
PREVIOUSLY OWNED
JUNK STATUS
©RAPID PHASE-2017 www.madamandeve.co.za

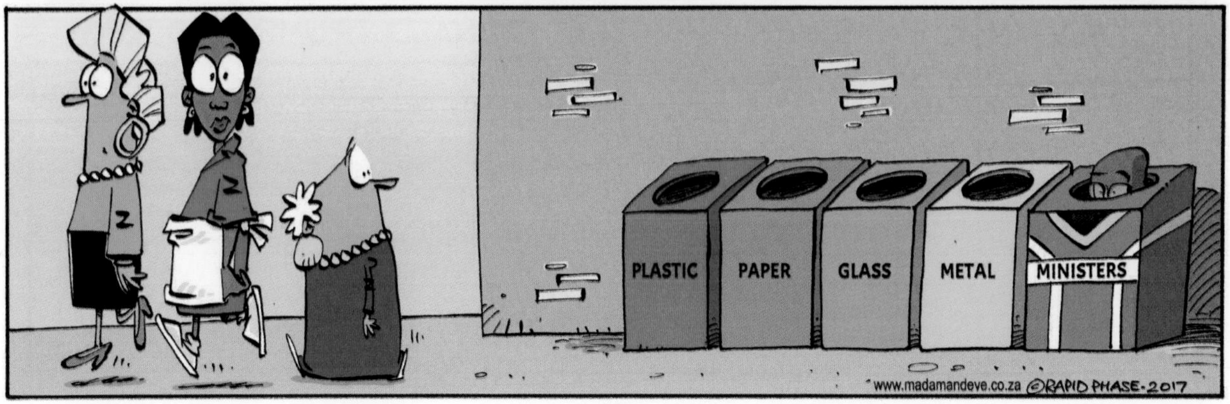
PLASTIC
PAPER
GLASS
METAL
MINISTERS
www.madamandeve.co.za ©RAPID PHASE-2017

Compared to *this*... saving the **GALAXY** was *easy*...

GUARDIANS OF THE TREASURY

INTRODUCING TWO GREAT NEW ICE CREAM FLAVOURS!

Haagen Donald **IMPEACH-MINT**

EXTREMELY **THICK** AND RICH!

"IT'S **UNBELIEVABLE!** SO GOOD, YOU'LL GET **TIRED OF EATING** ICE CREAM! AND THAT'S NO **FAKE NEWS!**"

BEN & JACOB's **BANANA REPUBLIC SPLIT**

CAPTURE A **TREASURY** OF TASTE!

"A NON-STOP **DOUBLE DIP!**"

WITH **ASSORTED NUTS!**

www.madamandeve.co.za

MADAM & EVE'S NEW PRESIDENT DONALD TRUMP EMOJIS

AWESOME! | UNVELIEVABLE! | SERIOUS | I LOVE THE CIA! | FAKE NEWS!! | NOBODY DOES BETTER THAN ME!

MORE PEOPLE AT MY INAUGURATION THAN ANY OTHER PRESIDENT! | DAMN DISHONEST MEDIA! | WINDY DAY | I AM PRESENTING "ALTERNATIVE FACTS" | I ♥ PUTIN! | WHERE'S MY HAIR STYLIST?

MADAM & Eve

BY STEPHEN FRANCIS & RICO

IN THE LIGHT OF THE MOON, A LITTLE EGG LAY ON A LEAF.

THE WARM SUN CAME UP... AND POP! OUT OF THE EGG CAME A TINY AND VERY HUNGRY ZUMAPILLAR!

HE WENT TO POLEKWANE AND ATE THABO MBEKI.

...BUT HE WAS STILL HUNGRY.

HE ATE THE CONSTITUTION.

HE ATE THE NKANDLA REPORT.

THEN HE ATE PRAVIN GORDHAN...

...AND THE RULE OF LAW.

HE WAS STILL HUNGRY.

HE ATE DIRECT FOREIGN INVESTMENT. ...HE ATE THE SABC, ESKOM, SAA... ...AND THE RAND.

HE WAS STILL HUNGRY.

HE ATE GWEDE MANTASHE.

HE ATE CYRIL RAMAPHOSA.

HE ATE THE WHOLE ANC.

AND SO THEN... HE ATE PRAVIN GORDHAN.

BUT HE WAS STILL HUNGRY.

TREASURY

© RAPID PHASE - 2017

HOLD ON!! HE ATE PRAVIN GORDHAN AGAIN?! FORGET IT! READ ME ANOTHER BOOK!

SIGH ...FINE.

READY? ..." GOODNIGHT MOON. GOODNIGHT TREASURY. GOODNIGHT DEMOCRACY. GOODNIGHT..."

MOM!!

LEGO MADAM &EVE

EVERYTHING IS AWESOME!

EVE! WHERE'S MY GIN & TONIC?!

WHAT A BUNCH OF BLOCKHEADS.

LEGO ZUMA

HEH. HEH. HEH.

THEY'LL NEVER REMOVE ME!

HOW CAN YOU BE SO SURE, SIR?

I GLUED MYSELF TO MY OFFICE FLOOR.

LEGO ZUMA

GUPTAS STATE CAPTURE SET

WATERKLOOF AIRBASE, ESKOM & SAXONWOLD SHEBEEN SETS SOLD SEPARATELY!

MADAM &EVE's KNOW YOUR BIRDS.

THE BLUEBIRD OF HAPPINESS

THE BLUEBIRD OF STUPIDITY

THE VULTURES OF OUTRAGE AND CONDEMNATION

MIELLLIES!

BZZZZZZZ

MIELLLIES!

BZZZZZZZ

HEE-HEE.

BZZZZZZZZZ

IS EVERYBODY USING ⑥#☆@ DRONES THESE DAYS?!

Ding! 🎵🎵

Sipho, your UBER BAKKIE driver has arrived.

"UBER BAKKIE?"

HI. I'M SIPHO. HOP ON!...JUST *IGNORE* THE OTHER TWO GUYS.

73

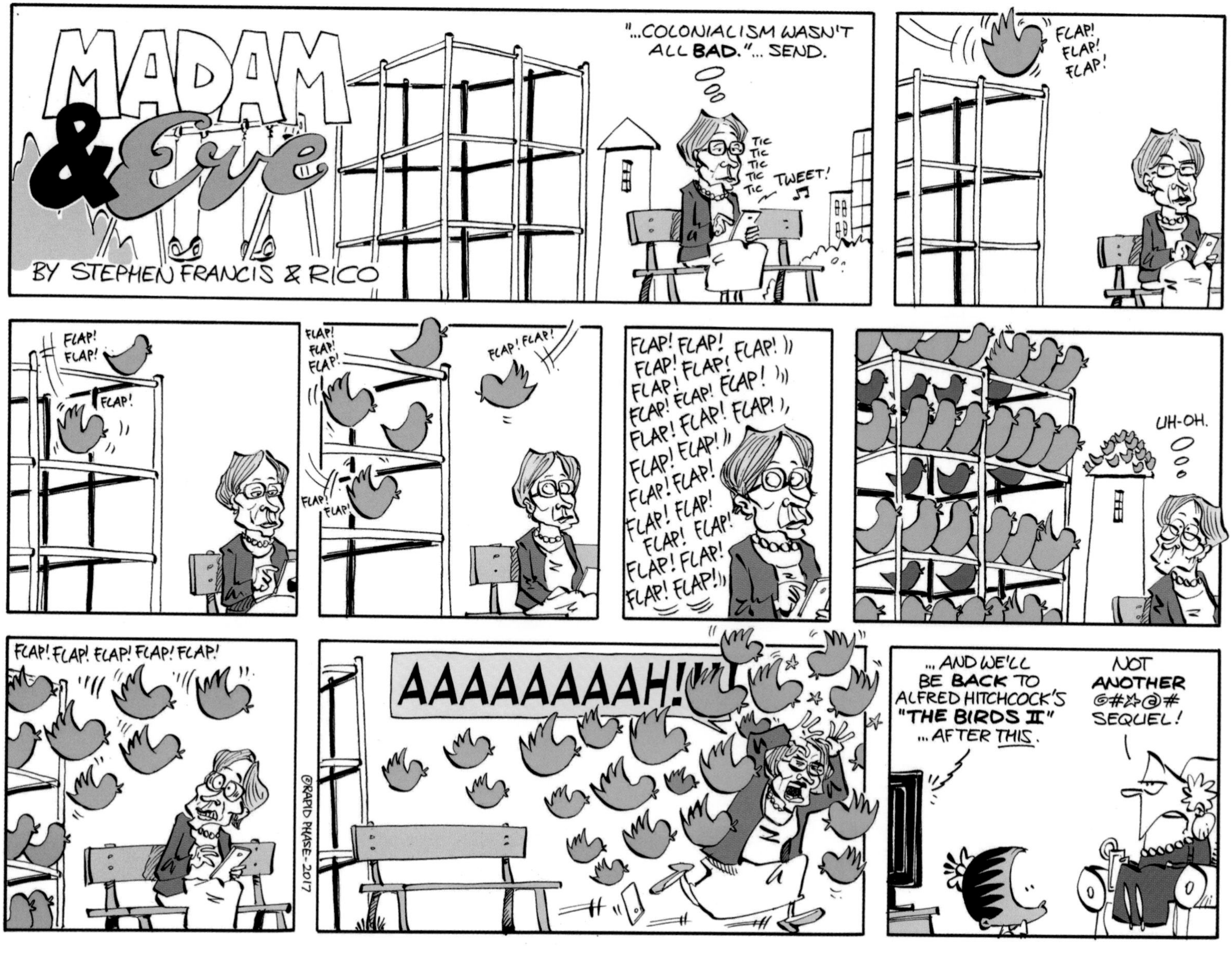
MADAM & Eve
BY STEPHEN FRANCIS & RICO
"...COLONIALISM WASN'T ALL BAD."... SEND.
TIC TIC TIC TIC TIC
TWEET!
FLAP! FLAP! FLAP!
FLAP! FLAP!
FLAP!
FLAP! FLAP! FLAP!
FLAP! FLAP!
FLAP! FLAP!
FLAP! FLAP!
UH-OH.
FLAP! FLAP! FLAP! FLAP! FLAP!
©RAPID PHASE-2017
AAAAAAAAH!!!
...AND WE'LL BE BACK TO ALFRED HITCHCOCK'S "THE BIRDS II" ...AFTER THIS.
NOT ANOTHER @#☆@# SEQUEL!

MADAM & Eve

BY STEPHEN FRANCIS & RICO

...ALTHOUGH IT'S BEEN DECIDED THAT WHATEVER WAS **DISCUSSED** DURING THE PRESIDENT ZUMA AND PRESIDENT TRUMP **TELECONFERENCE**... WILL REMAIN A MATTER OF **NATIONAL SECURITY**.

PRESIDENT TRUMP... PRESIDENT **ZUMA** ON LINE 3.

"...SAWYER BONER."
"SAWABONIA."
"SAWU..."
AH, THE **HELL** WITH IT.

JACOB! HOW'S EVERYTHING IN **NORTH AFRICA?**

I'M IN **SOUTH AFRICA!**

THERE'S **MORE THAN ONE?**

SO. WHAT DO YOU WANT TO DISCUSS?

I DON'T KNOW. WHAT DO **YOU** WANT TO DISCUSS?

I ASKED YOU **FIRST!**

OKAY. FINE! HOW MUCH **U.S. AID** DO YOU WANT?

LET'S SEE. UH... ELEVENTY- SEVEN MILLION... UH... LISTEN PROPERLY... UH... SEVEN...

G#☆@! JUST PUT IT INTO MY PERSONAL **BANK ACCOUNT!** I'LL TAKE IT FROM THERE!

AWESOME!

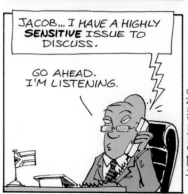

JACOB... I HAVE A HIGHLY **SENSITIVE** ISSUE TO DISCUSS.

GO AHEAD. I'M LISTENING.

©RAPID PHASE 2017

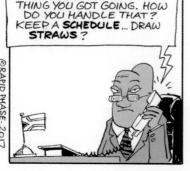

THAT WHOLE "FOUR WIVES" THING YOU GOT GOING. HOW DO YOU HANDLE THAT? KEEP A **SCHEDULE**... DRAW **STRAWS?**

NOT SO FAST! WHERE ARE ALL THOSE "**IVANKA MERCHANDISE** CARE PACKAGES" YOU **PROMISED** ME?!

I SENT THEM LAST WEEK! **NOBODY** SENDS MAIL BETTER THAN **ME!**

YOU SENT THEM THROUGH THE **SOUTH AFRICAN POST OFFICE?!** ARE YOU **CRAZY?!**

TIC. TIC. TIC. TIC.

HEY! ARE YOU **TWEETING?!**

UH-OH.

TIC. TIC. TIC.

LOOK AT THOSE POOR **AMERICANS**! STUCK WITH **DONALD TRUMP** AS THEIR **PRESIDENT**!

UP NEXT... PRESIDENT **ZUMA'S** STATE OF THE NATION.

YES, MISTER PRESIDENT?

TELL ME: WHERE DID **DONALD TRUMP** GET THE NICKNAME "**POTUS?**"

UH... IT STANDS FOR "PRESIDENT OF THE UNITED STATES."

SO MY NICKNAME WOULD BE...

WE COULD CALL YOU ..."**POSA**."

"POSA."

...YOU MEAN LIKE **RAMAPHOSA**?!!

UH-OH.

HELLO?

JACOB! HOW'S IT GOING, **BALDY**?

IS THAT YOUR NOSE ...OR ARE YOU EATING A **BANANA**?

EXCUSE ME?

WELL, GOTTA GO! NICE **TALKING** TO YA! HAR! HAR! :CLICK!:

...**TRUMP**. HE'S REALLY TRYING TO **PROVOKE** WORLD LEADERS.

@#✳@)!!

ATTENTION SANDF SOLDIERS!

DON'T JUST PROTECT SONA AND PARLIAMENT!

PROTECT YOUR BREATH TOO!

...with **DEPLOY-MINTS**

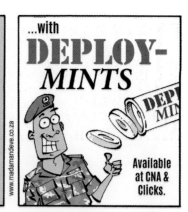

Available at CNA & Clicks.

THE FOLLOWING PROGRAMME CONTAINS **DISTURBING** SCENES OF **VIOLENCE** AND **STRONG LANGUAGE.**

SENSITIVE VIEWER DISCRETION IS ADVISED.

WHAT ARE YOU WATCHING?

HIGHLIGHTS OF **SONA 2017.**

POINT OF ORDER! MADAM SPEAKER! POINT OF ORDER!

"POINT OF ORDER!" "EXECUTIVE ORDER!"

ALL YOU HEAR THESE DAYS ARE **ORDERS!** ORDERS! **ORDERS!!**

WHAT ARE YOU DOING OUTSIDE? GOGO ORDER.

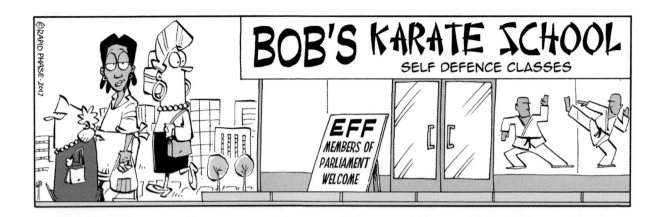

BOB'S KARATE SCHOOL
SELF DEFENCE CLASSES

EFF
MEMBERS OF PARLIAMENT WELCOME

POLICE COMMISSIONERS VS PRIVATE INVESTIGATORS	UNDERCOVER OPERATIVES VS UNDERCOVER OPERATIVES	URGENT INTERDICTS VS URGENT INTERDICTS	NEW SERIES: LAW& DISORDER Coming soon to SABC! (TV Executive vs TV Executive)

TODAY'S TOP STORY... **PRESIDENT TRUMP** HELD A **TELECONFERENCE** WITH **PRESIDENT ZUMA** ON THE SUBJECT OF "BILATERAL RELATIONS."

PRESIDENT ZUMA?

PRESIDENT TRUMP?

WHAT'S YOUR OPINION ON **BILATERAL** RELATIONSHIPS?

I'M ALL **FOR** THEM.

...AS LONG AS THEY DON'T GET **MARRIED** ...OR VOTE **AGAINST** ME.

I TOTALLY **AGREE.**

MADAM & Eve

BY STEPHEN FRANCIS & RICO

RELATIONS BETWEEN **PRESIDENT ZUMA** AND **CYRIL RAMAPHOSA** ARE SO **BAD**, IT IS RUMOURED THEY'RE BARELY **SPEAKING**... AND ARE SEEKING **MEDIATION**. THE IDENTITY OF THE MEDIATOR, HOWEVER, REMAINS A **MYSTERY**...

OKAY, GENTLEMEN. LET'S **BEGIN** WHO WANTS TO GO **FIRST?** ... **CYRIL?**

HEY! I'M THE **PRESIDENT!** ... I SHOULD GO FIRST!

SEE?! THIS IS WHAT I HAVE TO **DEAL** WITH! "I'M THE **PRESIDENT!**" I'M THE **PRESIDENT!**"

TELL HIM... I AM THE PRESIDENT!

THEN TELL HIM HE'S ALWAYS SENDING ME ON SILLY INTERNATIONAL TRIPS TO GET ME **OUT** OF THE WAY!

...TELL HIM THAT'S HIS **DUTY** AS **DEPUTY!!**

TELL HIM HE'S TRYING TO DISTRACT ME FROM MY OWN CAMPAIGNING!

TELL HIM NOT TO BE SUCH A **BABY!**

THEN TELL HIM HE PROMISED ME I'D BE THE NEXT PRESIDENT! ...AND NOW HE'S SUPPORTING HIS **EX-WIFE!**

THEN TELL HIM... I ALWAYS SAID WE SHOULD SEE **OTHER** PEOPLE!

WHAT DID THAT WOMAN PROMISE YOU?! --AMNESTY FROM THOSE CORRUPTION CHARGES?!

GENTLE-MEN, PLEASE!

www.madamandeve.co.za

©RAPID PHASE · 2017

ISN'T IT TIME WE **DISCUSS** THE **ELEPHANT** IN THE ROOM?

ELEPHANT? **WHAT** ELEPHANT?

RIGHT IN **FRONT** OF YOU! CAN'T YOU SEE IT?

THIS IS THE LAST TIME I TAKE ONE OF THESE **POLITICAL** MEDIATION JOBS.

HOW CAN I SEE **ANYTHING** WITH YOU ALWAYS HOGGING THE LIMELIGHT?!

RIBBIT! RIBBIT!

RIBBIT! RIBBIT!

GWEN! THERE'S A FROG IN THE LOUNGE!

RIBBIT! RIBBIT!

OH GOOD. I WAS LOOKING ALL OVER FOR IT!

RIBBIT! RIBBIT!

WHAT...DO I HAVE TO SEND YOU A MEMO EVERY TIME I CHANGE MY RINGTONE?

RIBBIT! RIBBIT!

RIBBIT! RIBBIT!

NOT AGAIN.

EVE!! TELL THANDI THAT IF SHE WANTS TO CHANGE HER RINGTONE TO A FROG, NOT TO LEAVE IT IN THE...

AAAAH!!

NOW WHAT?

HEY-- WHAT'S SHAKING WITH YOUR #WORLDVIEW?

IN TERMS OF OUR #ORGANISATIONALDNA, I THOUGHT IT WAS TIME TO #ONBOARD A LITTLE #BLUESKY.

TELL YOU WHAT: LET'S #PARK THAT FOR NOW... EVERYTHING'S #ONPOINT.

IT WAS GOOD #REACHINGOUT. I'M GLAD I GOT THIS #OFFMYCHEST.

#WORDS CAN'T DESCRIBE.

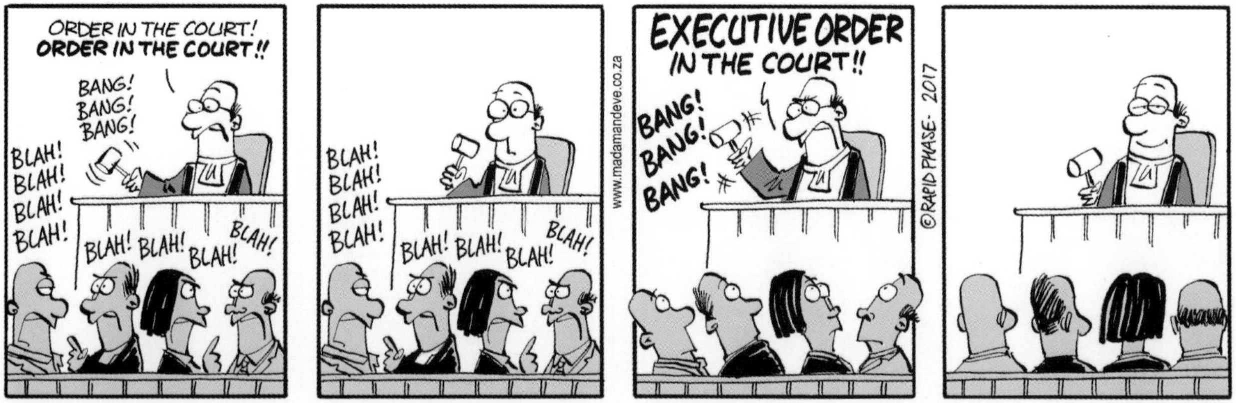
ORDER IN THE COURT! **ORDER IN THE COURT!!**
BANG! BANG! BANG!
BLAH! BLAH! BLAH! BLAH!
BLAH! BLAH! BLAH! BLAH!
BLAH! BLAH! BLAH! BLAH!
BLAH! BLAH! BLAH! BLAH!
www.madamandeve.co.za
EXECUTIVE ORDER IN THE COURT!!
BANG! BANG! BANG!
©RAPID PHASE · 2017

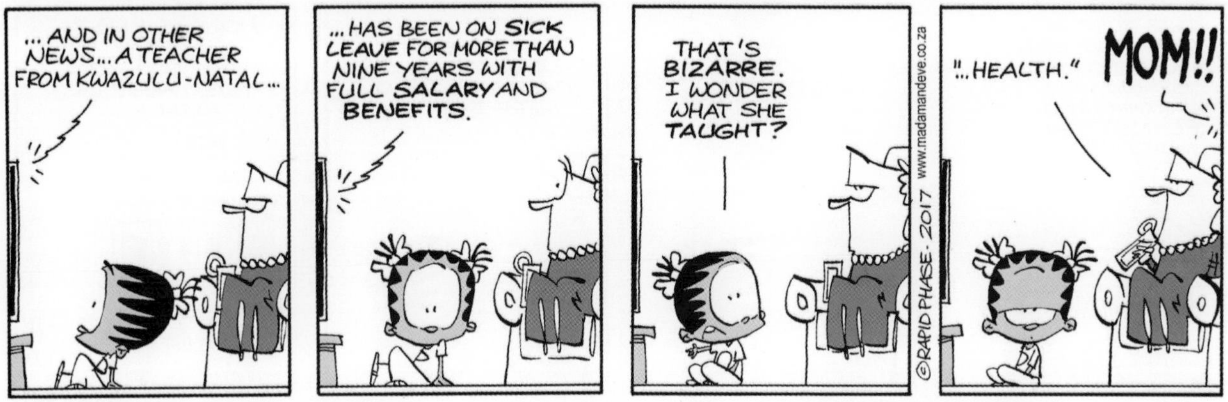
...AND IN OTHER NEWS... A TEACHER FROM KWAZULU-NATAL...
...HAS BEEN ON **SICK LEAVE** FOR MORE THAN NINE YEARS WITH FULL **SALARY** AND **BENEFITS**.
THAT'S **BIZARRE**. I WONDER WHAT SHE **TAUGHT**?
"...HEALTH."
MOM!!
©RAPID PHASE · 2017 www.madamandeve.co.za

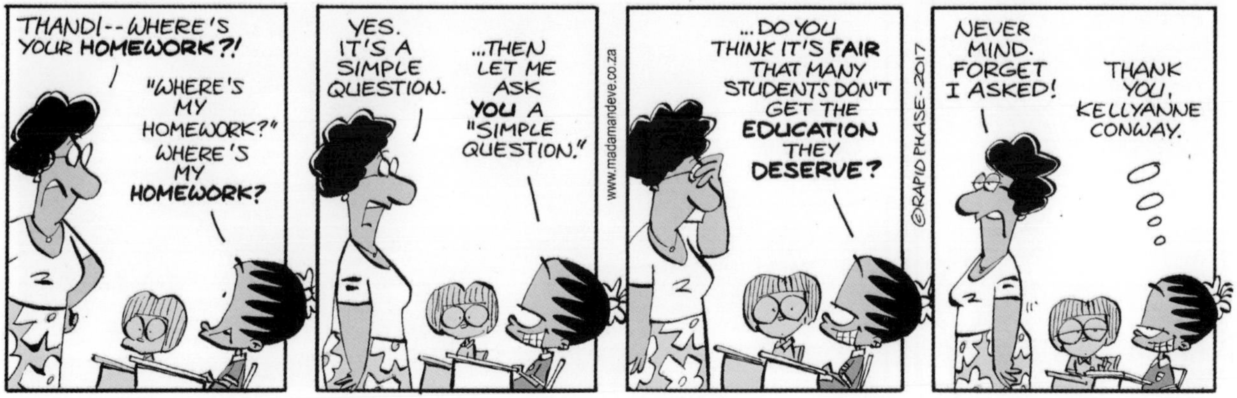
THANDI--WHERE'S YOUR **HOMEWORK?!**
"WHERE'S MY HOMEWORK?" WHERE'S MY **HOMEWORK?**
YES. IT'S A SIMPLE QUESTION.
...THEN LET ME ASK **YOU** A "SIMPLE QUESTION."
www.madamandeve.co.za
...DO YOU THINK IT'S **FAIR** THAT MANY STUDENTS DON'T GET THE **EDUCATION** THEY **DESERVE?**
©RAPID PHASE · 2017
NEVER MIND. FORGET I ASKED!
THANK YOU, KELLYANNE CONWAY.

AND IN OTHER NEWS, **SCIENTISTS** HAVE DISCOVERED A SERIES OF **PLANETS** THAT COULD SUPPORT **ALIEN LIFE**. REACTIONS ARE COMING IN THE WORLD OVER.

MADONNA

I'M ADOPTING **TWO** OF THEM! MAYBE **THREE**!

THE GUPTAS

ENOUGH "STATE CAPTURE"... TIME FOR "PLANET CAPTURE."

SAXONWOLD

BRIAN MOLEFE

THERE MUST BE A **SHEBEEN** THERE... I KNOW IT!

THIS JUST IN... **ASTRONOMERS** HAVE DISCOVERED **SEVEN** NEW EARTH-SIZED **PLANETS** IN A NEARBY SOLAR SYSTEM...

...THAT CAN SUPPORT **ALIEN LIFE**.

REACTIONS FROM **LEADERS** ALL OVER THE WORLD WERE **SWIFT**.

MORE ALIENS? @#☆@#!! WE'RE GOING TO NEED ANOTHER WALL!

CORRUPTION, CRIME, DROUGHT, UNEMPLOYMENT, POVERTY, HIGHER TAXES, EDUCATION CRISIS, JUNK STATUS, XENOPHOBIA, TERRORISM, CLIMATE CHANGE, WAR, TRUMP, ZUMA... WHAT **ELSE**...

...COULD POSSIBLY GO **WRONG** IN **2017**?!

MADAM & Eve

BY STEPHEN FRANCIS & RICO

TODAY'S TOP STORY: A DARING ARMED **ROBBERY** AT OR TAMBO **AIRPORT.** ALTHOUGH THE THIEVES **ESCAPED** WITH MILLIONS...

POLICE ARE NOW LOOKING FOR THE CRIMINAL **MASTERMIND** BEHIND THE HEIST... PRAVIN GORDHAN.

HUH?!

THIS JUST IN... **MINISTER DLAMINI** SAYS THAT THE **SASSA GRANT PAYMENTS** MAY NOT BE MADE ON TIME, DUE TO MISTAKES BY **PRAVIN GORDHAN.**

IN INTERNATIONAL NEWS... **PRESIDENT TRUMP** NOW CLAIMS THAT IT WASN'T THE **RUSSIANS** THAT HACKED U.S. COMPUTERS, BUT **PRAVIN GORDHAN.**

COMING UP... TONIGHT'S MOVIE: "THE EMPIRE STRIKES BACK?"

LUKE! TRUST YOUR FEELINGS. IT IS ME, **PRAVIN GORDHAN.**

WOW.

DON'T **BELIEVE** IT. IT'S ALL **FAKE NEWS!**

THERE'S A FACTION IN THE **ANC GOVERNMENT** THAT WANTS TO **BLAME** EVERYTHING ON THE **MINISTER** OF FINANCE.

©RAPID PHASE · 2017

IT'S UP TO **US** TO DISPEL THESE "**ALTERNATIVE FACTS**" WHENEVER YOU **CAN.**

GOTCHA.

THANDI -- ARE YOU SAYING YOUR **DOG** ATE YOUR HOMEWORK?

WELL, IT SURE AS HECK WASN'T **PRAVIN GORDHAN!**

MY **TEACHER** WANTS TO **TALK** WITH YOU.

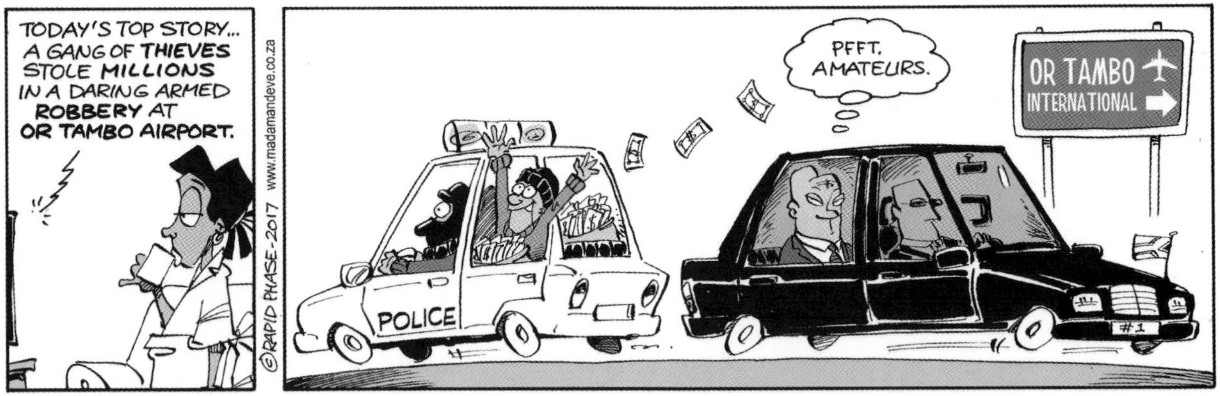
TODAY'S TOP STORY... A GANG OF THIEVES STOLE MILLIONS IN A DARING ARMED ROBBERY AT OR TAMBO AIRPORT.
©RAPID PHASE-2017 www.madamandeve.co.za
POLICE
PFFT. AMATEURS.
OR TAMBO INTERNATIONAL
#1

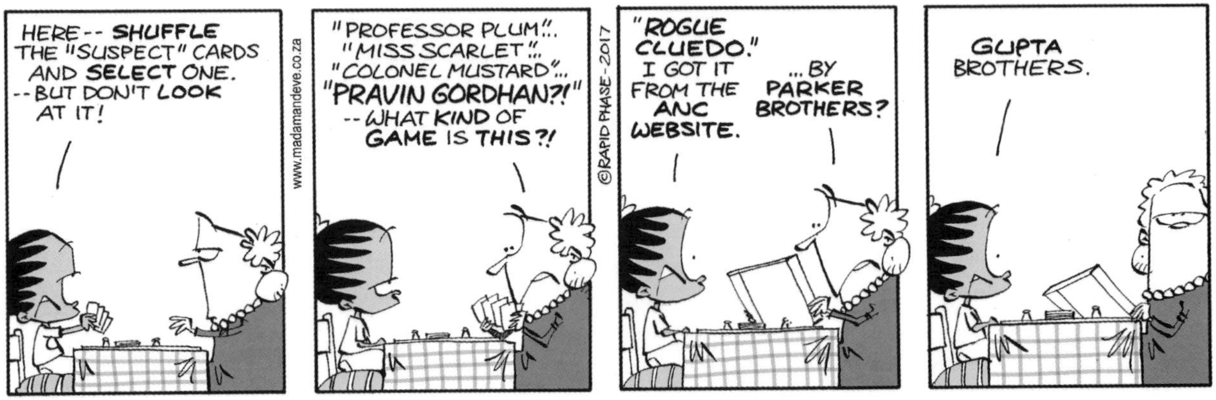
HERE-- SHUFFLE THE "SUSPECT" CARDS AND SELECT ONE. --BUT DON'T LOOK AT IT!
www.madamandeve.co.za
"PROFESSOR PLUM"... "MISS SCARLET"... "COLONEL MUSTARD"... "PRAVIN GORDHAN?!" --WHAT KIND OF GAME IS THIS?!
©RAPID PHASE-2017
"ROGUE CLUEDO." I GOT IT FROM THE ANC WEBSITE.
...BY PARKER BROTHERS?
GUPTA BROTHERS.

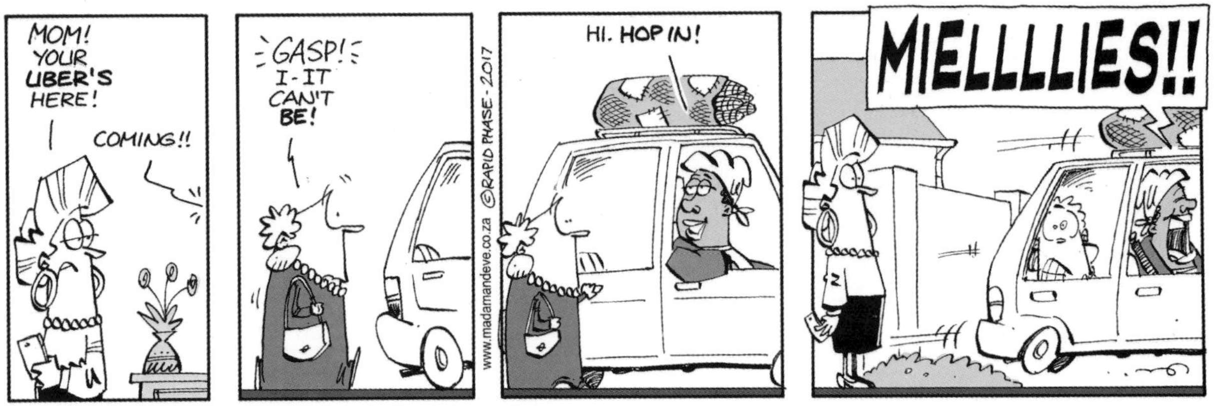
MOM! YOUR UBER'S HERE!
COMING!!
GASP! I-IT CAN'T BE!
©RAPID PHASE-2017
www.madamandeve.co.za
HI. HOP IN!
MIELLLLIES!!

WHAT IS YOUR WISH?

GENIE -- HERE IS A MAP OF AFRICA. I WANT ALL OF ITS PEOPLE TO LIVE IN PEACE AND HARMONY.

ALL OF AFRICA? THAT IS AN EXTREMELY DIFFICULT WISH! YOU HAVE ANYTHING EASIER?

OK...THEN I WISH MINISTER DLAMINI KEEPS HER PROMISE... AND THAT ALL SOCIAL GRANT PAYMENTS GO OUT ON APRIL 1st.

©RAPID PHASE - 2017

www.madamandeve.co.za

...LEMME SEE THAT @#*@ MAP AGAIN.

OKAY, THANDI. WHY DON'T YOU HAVE YOUR HOMEWORK ASSIGNMENT?

BECAUSE OF CLIMATE CHANGE.

CLIMATE CHANGE?!

EXACTLY.

©RAPID PHASE - 2017

YES... I WAS TOO BUSY WATCHING VIDEOS OF DURBAN BEACHFRONT FLOODING AND CYCLISTS BEING BLOWN AWAY BY CAPE TOWN WINDS!

www.madamandeve.co.za

MY TEACHER'S A CLIMATE CHANGE DENIER!!

GREAT STEW, EVE.

THANK YOU.

ALTHOUGH... YOU MIGHT HAVE TO WASH THE TABLECLOTH AFTER.

©RAPID PHASE - 2017

www.madamandeve.co.za

YEBO. IT REMINDS ME OF A BEST-SELLING NOVEL.

FIFTY SHADES OF GRAVY.

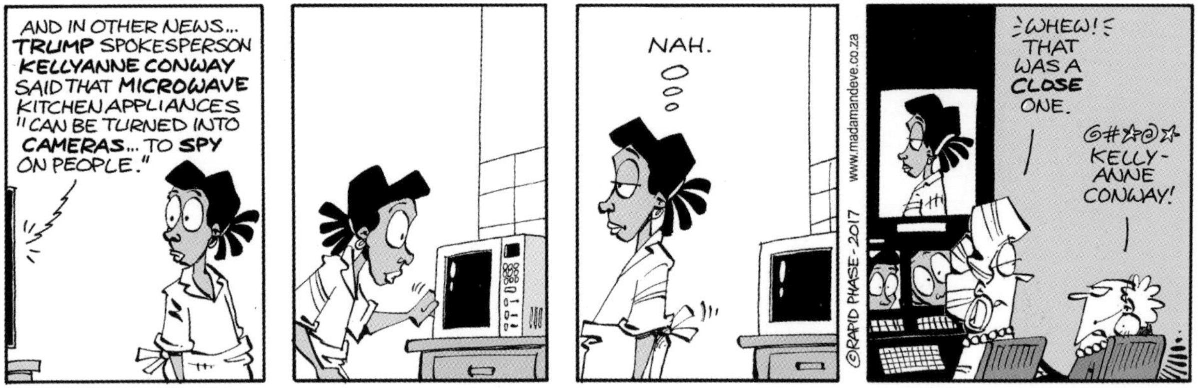
AND IN OTHER NEWS... TRUMP SPOKESPERSON KELLYANNE CONWAY SAID THAT MICROWAVE KITCHEN APPLIANCES "CAN BE TURNED INTO CAMERAS... TO SPY ON PEOPLE."
NAH.
WHEW! THAT WAS A CLOSE ONE.
@#☆@☆ KELLY-ANNE CONWAY!
©RAPID PHASE-2017
www.madamandeve.co.za

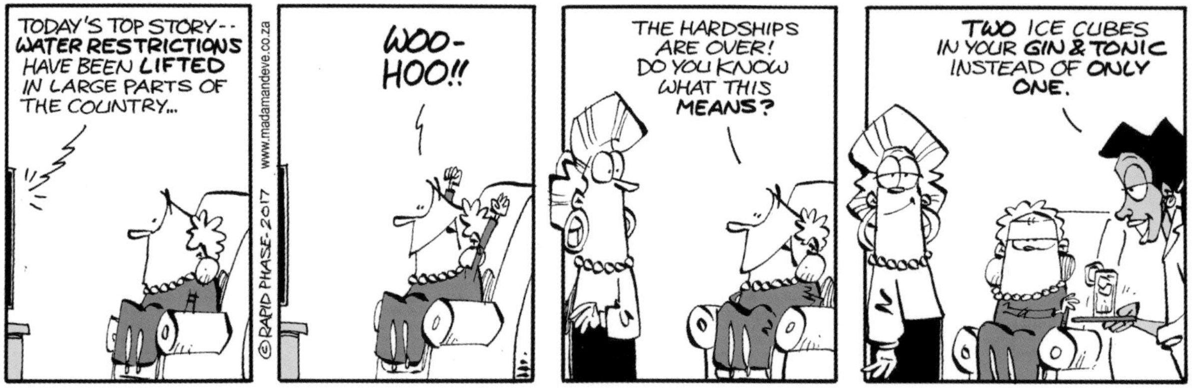
TODAY'S TOP STORY-- WATER RESTRICTIONS HAVE BEEN LIFTED IN LARGE PARTS OF THE COUNTRY...
©RAPID PHASE-2017
www.madamandeve.co.za
WOO-HOO!!
THE HARDSHIPS ARE OVER! DO YOU KNOW WHAT THIS MEANS?
TWO ICE CUBES IN YOUR GIN & TONIC INSTEAD OF ONLY ONE.

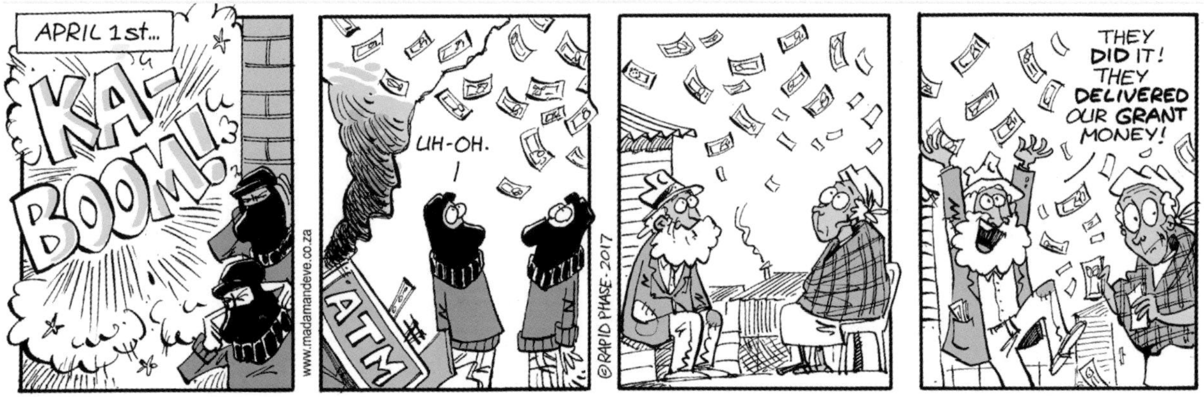
APRIL 1st...
KA-BOOM!
www.madamandeve.co.za
UH-OH.
ATM
©RAPID PHASE-2017
THEY DID IT! THEY DELIVERED OUR GRANT MONEY!

MADAM & Eve

BY STEPHEN FRANCIS & RICO

RIGHT. OKAY, THANDI. WHERE'S YOUR HOMEWORK?

I HAVE A PREPARED STATEMENT.

SIGH

AHEM.

"CERTAIN OPPOSING ELEMENTS BELIEVE THAT THERE IS A CRISIS WHEN IT COMES TO ME HANDING IN MY HOMEWORK."

©RAPID PHASE · 2017

"THIS IS MERE SELF-SERVING PROPAGANDA..."

"...AND GRANDSTANDING OF THE HIGHEST ORDER!"

"THESE 'SCARE TACTICS' FROM THESE PROPHETS OF DOOM... MUST STOP!"

"THEREFORE... LET ME REITERATE MY ASSURANCE!"

"...THERE IS NO CRISIS!!"

THANK YOU.

GOOD! THEN WHERE'S YESTERDAY'S HOMEWORK?

I'LL HAND IT IN ON APRIL 1st.

SHE KICKED YOU OUT?

I'VE BECOME A POLITICAL FOOTBALL.

PRINCIPAL

CYRIL RAMAPHOSA SAID: "WE ARE A NATION THAT DOES NOT BUILD **WALLS**. WE DO **NOT** BELIEVE IN BUILDING WALLS."

REALLY?

...COULD'VE FOOLED ME.

FIRST STRIKE
ARMED RESPONSE

www.madamandeve.co.za

© RAPID PHASE - 2017

AND IN OTHER NEWS... SOUTH AFRICA HAS **BANNED** MEAT IMPORTS FROM BRAZIL OVER A **ROTTEN MEAT** SCANDAL...

BEEF STEAK CUTS

RUMP

PORTERHOUSE

T-BONE

BRAZILIAN

www.madamandeve.co.za

© RAPID PHASE - 2017

I KNOW WHAT YOU'RE **THINKING**. "DID SHE SPRITZ **SIX** TIMES... OR ONLY **FIVE**?" BUT BEING THIS IS **DOOM**... THE MOST **POWERFUL** BUG SPRAY AROUND...

... YOU HAVE TO ASK YOURSELF A **QUESTION**: "DO I FEEL LUCKY?" WELL, **DO YA**, PUNK?!

© RAPID PHASE - 2017   www.madamandeve.co.za

AAAAH!!

SPROING!!

HISS!

I HATE PARKTOWN PRAWNS.

SPROING!

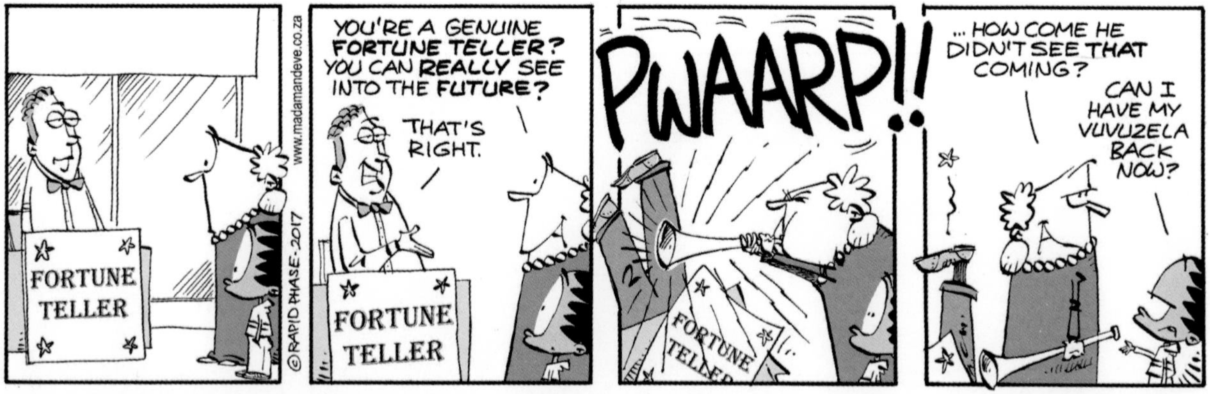
FORTUNE TELLER
©RAPID PHASE·2017
www.madamandeve.co.za
YOU'RE A GENUINE **FORTUNE TELLER**? YOU CAN **REALLY** SEE INTO THE **FUTURE**?
THAT'S RIGHT.
FORTUNE TELLER
PWAARP!!
... HOW COME HE DIDN'T SEE **THAT** COMING?
CAN I HAVE MY VUVUZELA BACK NOW?

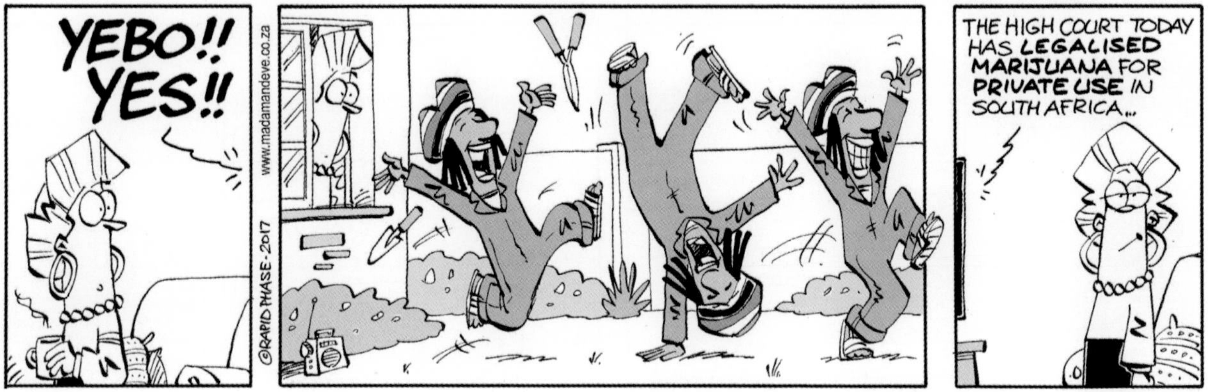
YEBO!! YES!!
©RAPID PHASE·2017
www.madamandeve.co.za
THE HIGH COURT TODAY HAS **LEGALISED MARIJUANA** FOR **PRIVATE USE** IN SOUTH AFRICA...

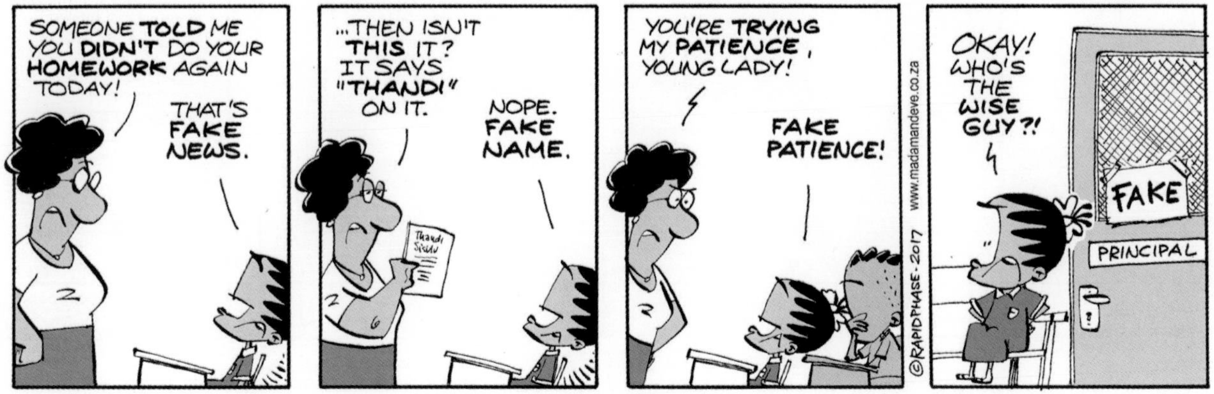
SOMEONE **TOLD** ME YOU **DIDN'T** DO YOUR **HOMEWORK** AGAIN TODAY!
THAT'S **FAKE NEWS**.
...THEN ISN'T **THIS** IT? IT SAYS "**THANDI**" ON IT.
NOPE. **FAKE NAME**.
YOU'RE **TRYING** MY **PATIENCE**, YOUNG LADY!
FAKE PATIENCE!
©RAPID PHASE·2017
www.madamandeve.co.za
OKAY! WHO'S THE **WISE GUY**?!
FAKE
PRINCIPAL

MADAM & Eve

BY STEPHEN FRANCIS & RICO

HELLO EVERYBODY! IT'S TIME TO PLAY SOUTH AFRICA'S NEWEST GAME SHOW...

HIRED ...OR FIRED?!

CLAP! CLAP! CLAP! CLAP! CLAP! CLAP! CLAP! CLAP! CLAP! CLAP! CLAP!

OUR SPECIAL GUEST FOR TODAY-- GIVE IT UP FOR FINANCE MINISTER PRAVIN GORDHAN!

CLAP! CLAP! CLAP! CLAP! CLAP! CLAP!

AUDIENCE--THE RAND IS FALLING, SO THERE'S NO TIME TO LOSE! IS PRAVIN HIRED... OR FIRED?!

VOTE NOW!!

Click! Click! Click! Click! Click! Click! Click!

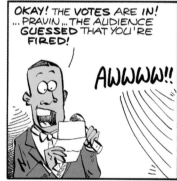

OKAY! THE VOTES ARE IN! ...PRAVIN... THE AUDIENCE GUESSED THAT YOU'RE FIRED!

AWWWW!!

PRAVIN... WHAT'S THE REAL TRUTH? TELL US!

ACTUALLY...

AS FAR AS I KNOW... I'M STILL HIRED.

HE'S STILL HIRED!!

YAY! CLAP! YAY! CLAP! CLAP! CLAP! CLAP! CLAP!

©RAPID PHASE 2017

THAT'S ALL FOR TODAY! JOIN US NEXT TIME ON "HIRED... OR FIRED!"

... WHEN OUR SPECIAL GUEST WILL BE HELEN ZILLE! GOODNIGHT EVERYBODY!

CLAP! CLAP! CLAP! CLAP! CLAP! CLAP! CLAP! CLAP! CLAP!

COMING UP NEXT... OUR NEW CABINET PROGRAMME: "SHUFFLE OR RESHUFFLE?!"

I LOVE GAME SHOW NIGHT!

Two days after this cartoon was published, Pravin Gordhan was fired by President Zuma in the now infamous cabinet reshuffle.

DING! DING! THERE'S THE BELL! BOTH OPPONENTS CIRCLE EACH OTHER WARILY.

AND **ZUMA** LEADS WITH A VICIOUS RIGHT **RECALL**. BUT **GORDHAN** COMES BACK WITH A COUNTER BLOW: "I WAS COMING BACK **ANYWAY!**"

ZUMA'S **DESPERATE!** HERE COMES HIS **DOUBLE CROSS!** HE'S THREATENING HIS FAMOUS **RESHUFFLE!**

OOH!! AND THE **RAND** TAKES A **HUGE HIT!** IT'S GOING **DOWN!**

I CAN'T **WATCH!** CALL ME WHEN IT'S OVER!

YES, MISTER PRESIDENT?

I JUST **FIRED** PRAVIN GORDHAN.

HAHAHA! GOOD ONE! APRIL FOOLS!

NO. REALLY. I JUST FIRED HIM.

HAHAHA! HOHOHO! APRIL FOOL! WE LOVE IT!!

AND I ALSO FIRED A BUNCH OF OTHER MINISTERS AS WELL!

BWAHAHAHA! STOP! HOO! HOO! YOU'RE KILLING US!

I'LL WAIT. YOU TWO ARE NEXT.

You're Number One.

So be <u>bold</u>.

Everybody knows the truth.

No point pretending any longer.

So reshuffle the cabinet and let the chips fall where they may.

But what do you care?

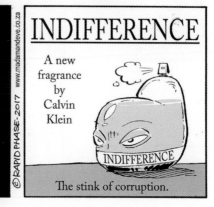

INDIFFERENCE

A new fragrance by Calvin Klein

INDIFFERENCE

The stink of corruption.

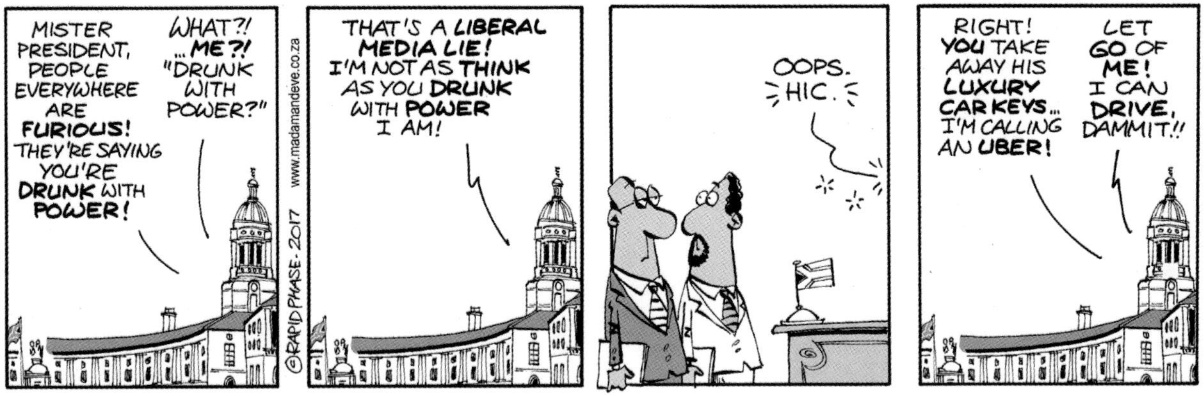
MISTER PRESIDENT, PEOPLE EVERYWHERE ARE FURIOUS! THEY'RE SAYING YOU'RE DRUNK WITH POWER!
WHAT?! ...ME?! "DRUNK WITH POWER?"
©RAPID PHASE-2017 www.madamandeve.co.za
THAT'S A LIBERAL MEDIA LIE! I'M NOT AS THINK AS YOU DRUNK WITH POWER I AM!
OOPS. HIC.
RIGHT! YOU TAKE AWAY HIS LUXURY CAR KEYS... I'M CALLING AN UBER!
LET GO OF ME! I CAN DRIVE, DAMMIT!!

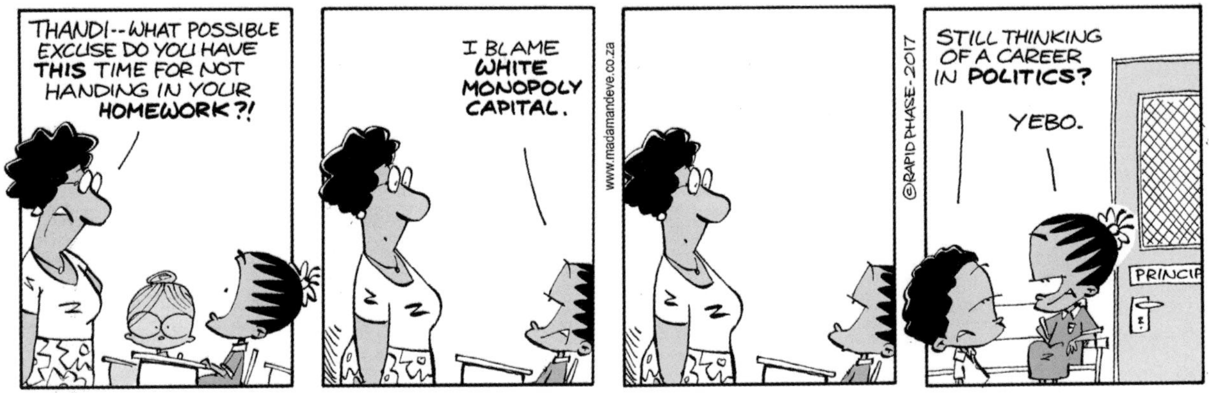
THANDI--WHAT POSSIBLE EXCUSE DO YOU HAVE THIS TIME FOR NOT HANDING IN YOUR HOMEWORK?!
I BLAME WHITE MONOPOLY CAPITAL.
www.madamandeve.co.za
©RAPID PHASE-2017
STILL THINKING OF A CAREER IN POLITICS?
YEBO.
PRINCIP

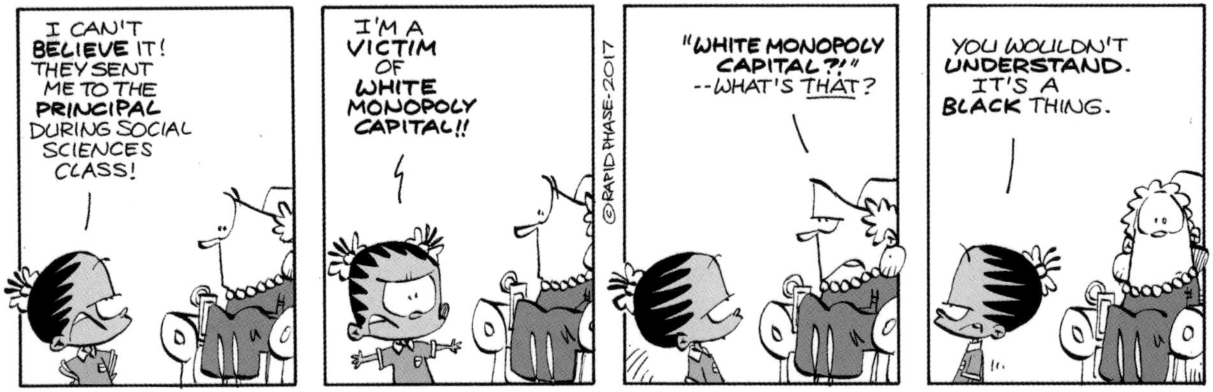
I CAN'T BELIEVE IT! THEY SENT ME TO THE PRINCIPAL DURING SOCIAL SCIENCES CLASS!
I'M A VICTIM OF WHITE MONOPOLY CAPITAL!!
©RAPID PHASE-2017
"WHITE MONOPOLY CAPITAL?!" --WHAT'S THAT?
YOU WOULDN'T UNDERSTAND. IT'S A BLACK THING.

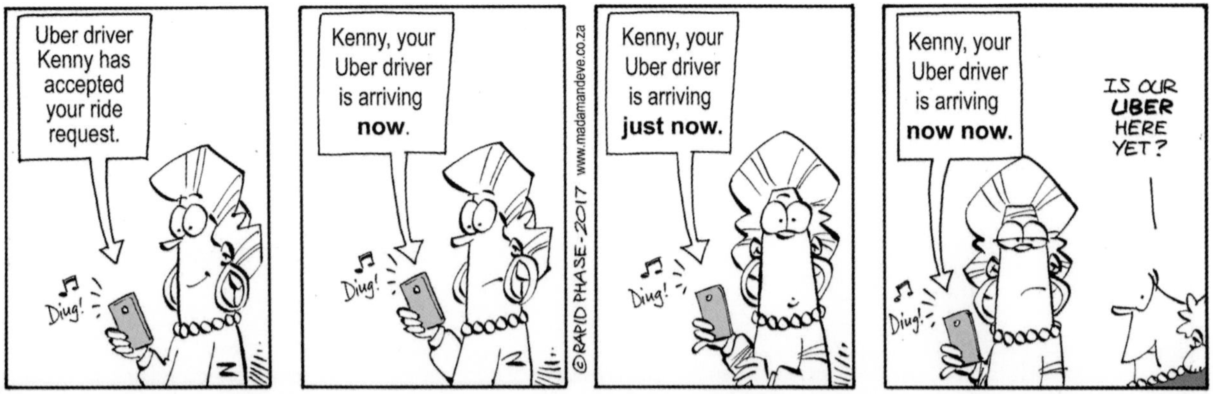
Uber driver Kenny has accepted your ride request.
Diug!
Kenny, your Uber driver is arriving **now**.
Diug!
©RAPID PHASE-2017 www.madamandeve.co.za
Kenny, your Uber driver is arriving **just now.**
Diug!
Kenny, your Uber driver is arriving **now now.**
Diug!
IS OUR **UBER** HERE YET?

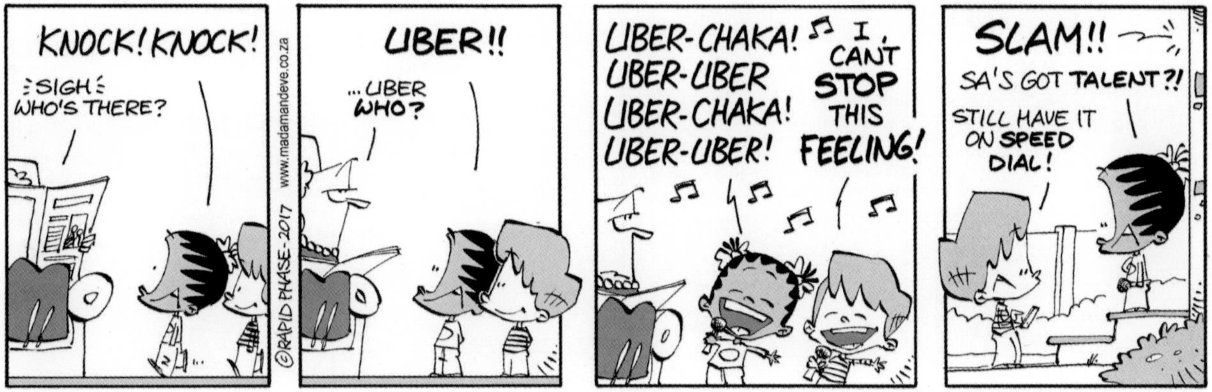
KNOCK! KNOCK!
SIGH WHO'S THERE?
©RAPID PHASE-2017 www.madamandeve.co.za
UBER!!
...UBER **WHO?**
UBER-CHAKA! UBER-UBER UBER-CHAKA! UBER-UBER!
I CAN'T **STOP** THIS **FEELING!**
SLAM!!
SA'S GOT **TALENT?!**
STILL HAVE IT ON **SPEED DIAL!**

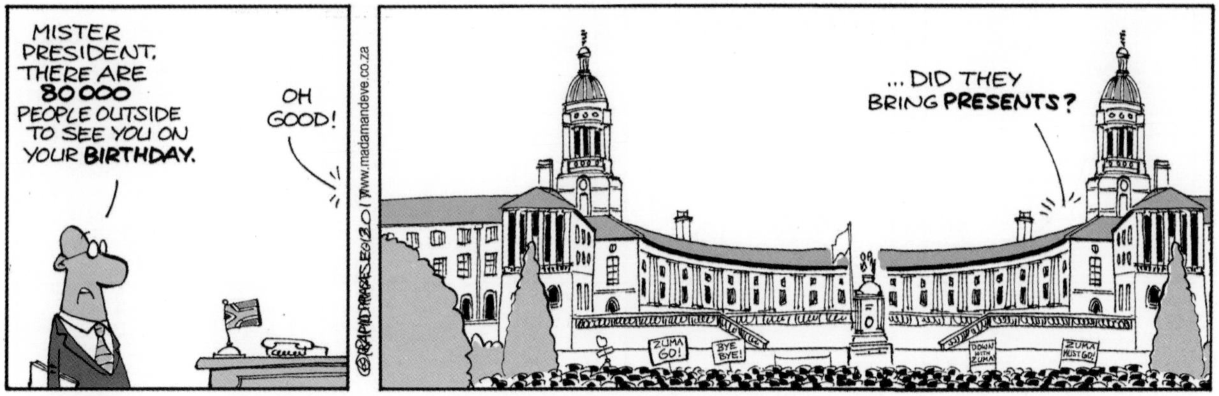
MISTER PRESIDENT, THERE ARE **80 000** PEOPLE OUTSIDE TO SEE YOU ON YOUR **BIRTHDAY.**
OH GOOD!
©RAPID PHASE-2017 www.madamandeve.co.za
...DID THEY BRING **PRESENTS?**
ZUMA GO!
BYE BYE!
DOWN WITH ZUMA
ZUMA MUST GO!

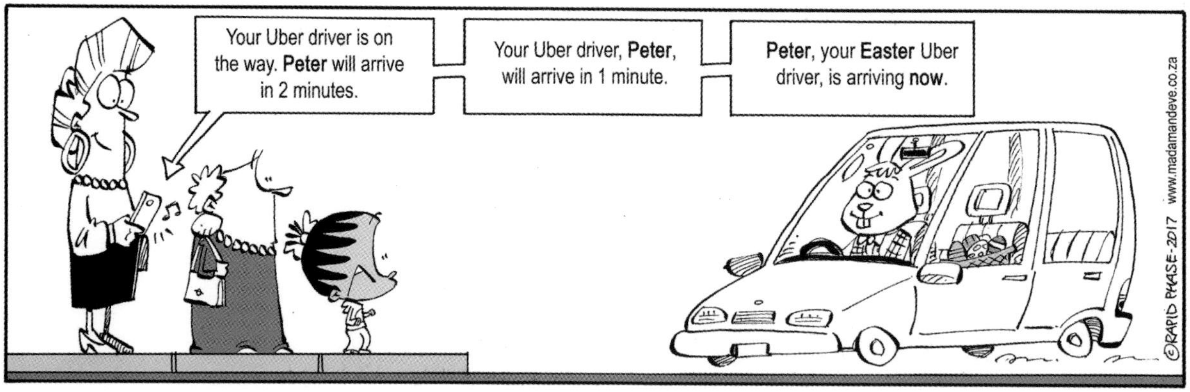
Your Uber driver is on the way. Peter will arrive in 2 minutes.
Your Uber driver, Peter, will arrive in 1 minute.
Peter, your Easter Uber driver, is arriving now.
©RAPID PHASE-2017 www.madamandeve.co.za

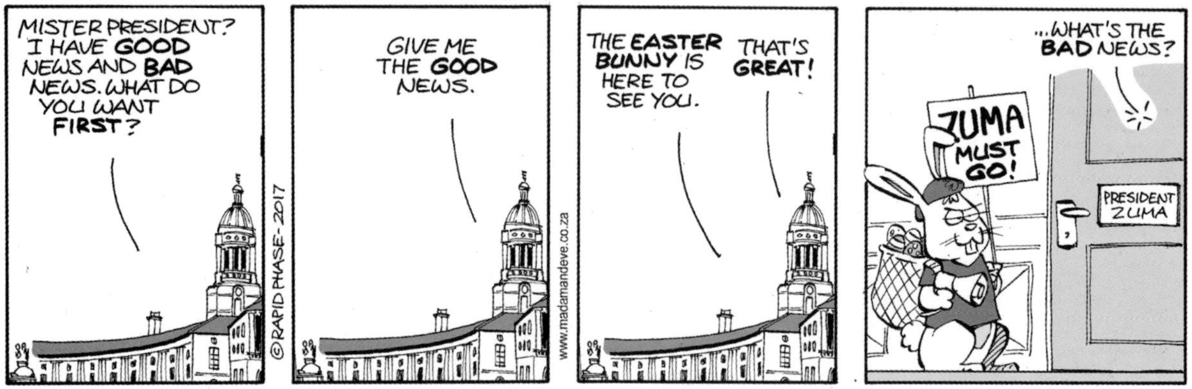
MISTER PRESIDENT? I HAVE GOOD NEWS AND BAD NEWS. WHAT DO YOU WANT FIRST?
©RAPID PHASE-2017
GIVE ME THE GOOD NEWS.
www.madamandeve.co.za
THE EASTER BUNNY IS HERE TO SEE YOU.
THAT'S GREAT!
...WHAT'S THE BAD NEWS?
ZUMA MUST GO!
PRESIDENT ZUMA

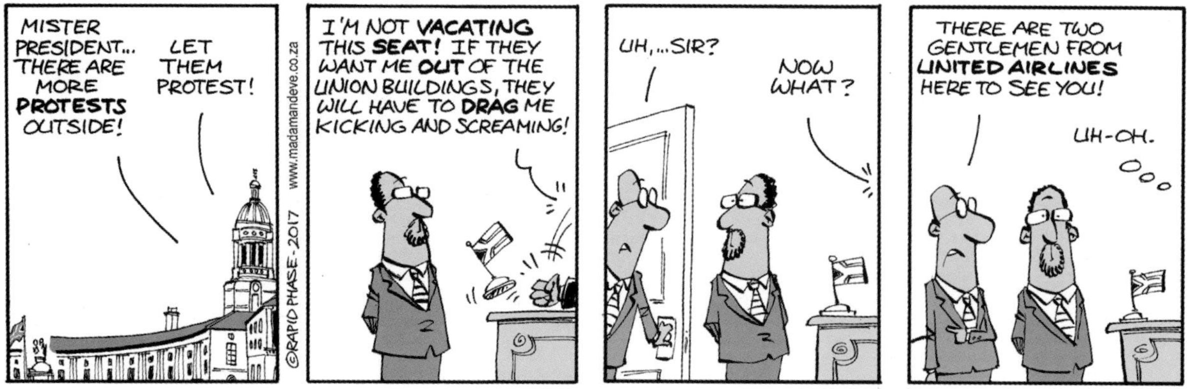
MISTER PRESIDENT... THERE ARE MORE PROTESTS OUTSIDE!
LET THEM PROTEST!
©RAPID PHASE-2017 www.madamandeve.co.za
I'M NOT VACATING THIS SEAT! IF THEY WANT ME OUT OF THE UNION BUILDINGS, THEY WILL HAVE TO DRAG ME KICKING AND SCREAMING!
UH,...SIR?
NOW WHAT?
THERE ARE TWO GENTLEMEN FROM UNITED AIRLINES HERE TO SEE YOU!
UH-OH.

MADAM & Eve

BY STEPHEN FRANCIS & RICO

Your Uber driver is on the way. Kenny will arrive in 10 minutes.

PLEASE TELL MOM "KENNY'S ON THE WAY!"

GOGO-- KENNY'S ON HIS WAY!

WHO THE HELL IS "KENNY"?

Your Uber driver, Kenny, is on his way. He will arrive in 8 minutes.

@RAPID PHASE-2017

Kenny, your Uber driver, will arrive in 5 minutes.

Kenny, your Uber driver, is hungry. After he picks up his takeaway, he will arrive in 9 minutes.

Kenny, your Uber driver, is in an altercation with a Spur customer. He will arrive in 5 minutes.

Kenny, your Uber driver, is delayed by a large anti-Zuma march. He will arrive in 10 minutes.

Kenny, your Uber driver, is further delayed due to a violent ANCYL pro-Zuma protest. He will arrive in 5 minutes.

Kenny, your Uber driver, will arrive **now now**.

Kenny, your Uber driver, will arrive **just now**.

Kenny, your Uber driver, is arriving now.

CRASH!

Kenny, your recently licensed Uber driver, just accidentally crashed into your electric gate.

Kenny, your Uber driver, is driving away quickly. He left you a Spur burger and chips.

IS OUR **UBER** DRIVER HERE YET?

GOLDEN RETRIEVER

GOLDEN RECEIVER

R30 MILLION

ESKOM

FASTER THAN EVER BEFORE.

WILDER THAN EVER BEFORE.

GET READY FOR THE RIDE OF YOUR LIFE.

FAST AND FURIOUS 9
MINIBUS OVERLOADED

Coming soon to a highway near you!

MARY HAD A LITTLE **LAMB**

IT'S FLEECE WAS WHITE AS SNOW

BAA!

SHE USED IT AS **COLLATERAL**

TO GET A NEW **BANK LOAN.**

BAA?

BANK MANAGER

AND IN OTHER NEWS... **ZIMBABWE** BANKS MAY SOON HAVE TO ACCEPT COWS, SHEEP AND OTHER **LIVESTOCK** AS SECURITY FOR CASH **LOANS.**

MADAM & Eve

BY STEPHEN FRANCIS & RICO

I KNOW WHAT I WANT TO BE WHEN I GROW UP! ...A RECEIVER.

A RECEIVER OF REVENUE?

A RECEIVER OF GOLDEN HANDSHAKES!

CHECK THIS OUT. SHAKE.

KER-CHING! THAT'S 30 MILLION BUCKS YOU OWE ME!

KER-CHING! THAT'S 40 MILLION! EASIEST JOB IN THE WHOLE WORLD!

AND WHAT EXACTLY DO YOU DO TO EARN A "GOLDEN HANDSHAKE?"

I HAVE TO DO SOMETHING?!!

THE GUYS IN THE NEWS DON'T SEEM TO DO ANYTHING EXCEPT QUIT.

©RAPID PHASE - 2017

www.madamandeve.co.za

AND WHAT IF THE ANC ISN'T STILL IN POWER WHEN I GROW UP? THAT COULD RUIN EVERYTHING!

WAIT! WHAT IF I START SMALL? HOW MUCH IS A SILVER HANDSHAKE?

GO PLAY.

AHEM
BEFORE WE BEGIN, I'D LIKE TO RECOMMEND A MOTION OF **NO CONFIDENCE** IN FUTURE **HOMEWORK!**

FURTHERMORE... I RECOMMEND IT BE A **SECRET BALLOT!**

I THINK SHE GUESSED WHICH WAY MY **VOTE** WOULD GO.

PRINCIP[AL]

HI.

DO YOU BELIEVE IN **RADICAL ECONOMIC TRANSFORMATION?**

SURE.

GOOD. **LOAN** ME **TWENTY BUCKS.**

...MAYBE THAT WAS A TAD **TOO** RADICAL.

LET'S SEE... "OMO... FEATHER DUSTER..."

"...CLEANING CLOTHS...MOP..."

WHAT ARE YOU DOING?

EVE SAID SHE'S WRITING A **"BUCKET LIST...** SO I OFFERED TO **HELP.**

YOU EXPLAIN IT. I'M ON MY **BREAK.**

MADAM & Eve

BY STEPHEN FRANCIS & RICO

ACCORDING TO SOURCES, **PRESIDENT ZUMA** IS GETTING INCREASINGLY **PARANOID**, WORRYING IF MEMBERS OF HIS INNER CIRCLE STILL **SUPPORT** HIM ONE **HUNDRED PERCENT**.

THE NEXT DEPUTY MINISTER IS HERE FOR HIS "**LOYALTY TEST**," MISTER PRESIDENT.

OH, GOODIE! SEND HIM IN!

ARE YOU STILL **LOYAL** TO PRESIDENT **ZUMA**?

ABSOLUTELY!!

THE **PRESIDENT** WANTS YOU TO **HOP** ON ONE **LEG** AND MAKE A **NOISE** LIKE A **CHICKEN**. GO!

PUK! PUK! PUK! PUK! PUK! PUK!

GOOD. NOW TAKE OFF YOUR SHOES AND WALK OVER THOSE **HOT COALS** WHILE SHOUTING **RADICAL ECONOMIC TRANSFORMATION!**

OW! OW! OW! **RADICAL**...OW! **ECO**...OW...NOMIC @#×@ OW! OW! **TRANSFORMATION!!**

STILL **LOYAL** TO PRESIDENT **ZUMA**?

YES!

GOOD. THE PRESIDENT WANTS YOU TO **HIT YOURSELF** ON THE HEAD WITH THIS **RUBBER MALLET** UNTIL HE TELLS YOU TO STOP.

©RAPID PHASE - 2017

HAVEN'T I PROVED MY LOYALTY **YET**?!

YOU PROVED YOUR **LOYALTY** FIVE MINUTES AGO. **NOW** WE'RE INTERVIEWING YOU FOR ALTERNATE **FINANCE MINISTER**.

BONK! OW!! **BONK!** OW!!

...WHAT DO YOU THINK, SIR?

I LIKE HIS **SPIRIT**. PUT HIM ON THE **SHORTLIST**.

...ANOTHER CABINET **RESHUFFLE.**

HMM... LET ME SEE... SWOP THE **ACE** AND THE **JOKER**...

A ♠ — 3 ♦ — J JOKER — 6 ♥

©RAPID PHASE - 2017

WHAT'S ALL **THIS**?

DON'T YOU **READ** THE **PAPERS**?! THE BIG **HIKE** IS ALMOST HERE!

YOU CAN **SPONSOR** US. ONLY **FIVE BUCKS** PER **LITRE.**

...YOU MEAN **FIVE BUCKS** PER **KILO-METER**?

www.madamandeve.co.za

NO, **LITRE.** IT'S THE **BIG PETROL** PRICE HIKE!

©RAPID PHASE - 2017

SLAM!!

INVESTOR CONFIDENCE IS **SHAKY** THESE DAYS.

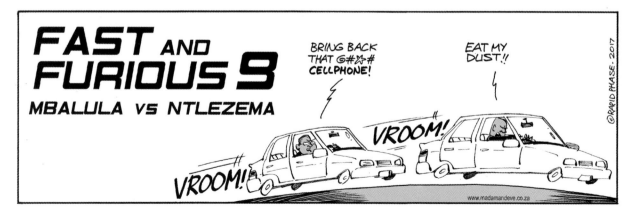

FAST AND FURIOUS 9
MBALULA VS NTLEZEMA

BRING BACK THAT @#✳# CELLPHONE!

EAT MY DUST!!

VROOM!

VROOM!

©RAPID PHASE - 2017

www.madamandeve.co.za

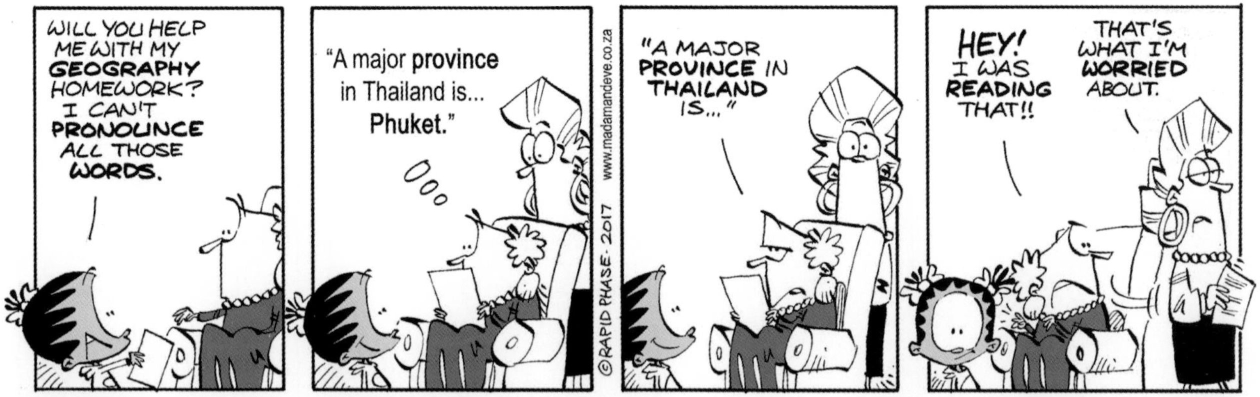
WILL YOU HELP ME WITH MY GEOGRAPHY HOMEWORK? I CAN'T PRONOUNCE ALL THOSE WORDS.
"A major province in Thailand is... Phuket."
www.madamandeve.co.za
©RAPID PHASE - 2017
"A MAJOR PROVINCE IN THAILAND IS..."
HEY! I WAS READING THAT!!
THAT'S WHAT I'M WORRIED ABOUT.

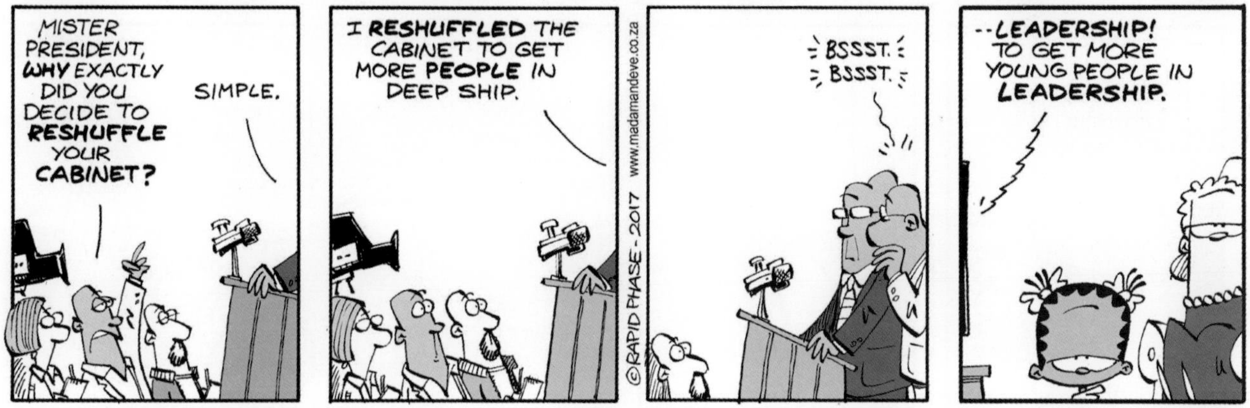
MISTER PRESIDENT, WHY EXACTLY DID YOU DECIDE TO RESHUFFLE YOUR CABINET?
SIMPLE.
I RESHUFFLED THE CABINET TO GET MORE PEOPLE IN DEEP SHIP.
www.madamandeve.co.za
©RAPID PHASE - 2017
BSSST. BSSST.
--LEADERSHIP! TO GET MORE YOUNG PEOPLE IN LEADERSHIP.

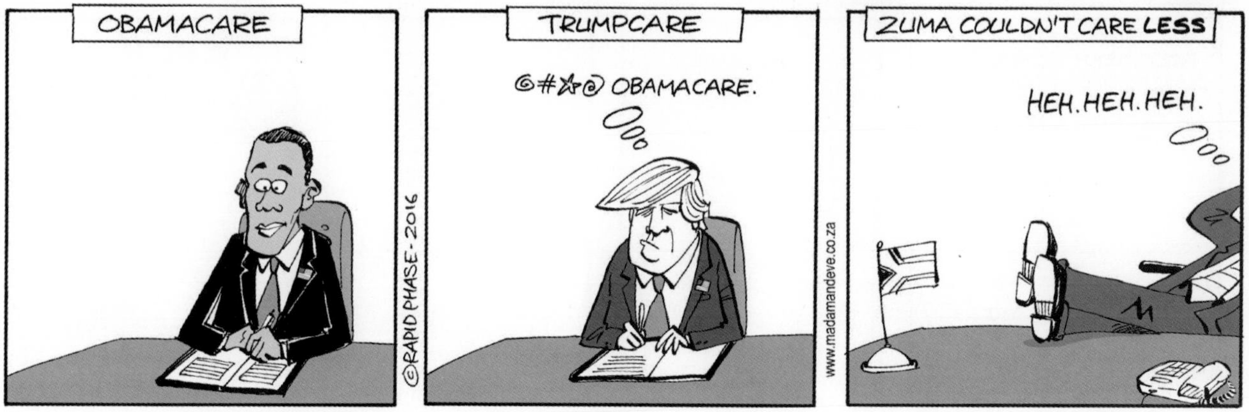
OBAMACARE
©RAPID PHASE - 2016
TRUMPCARE
@#☆@ OBAMACARE.
www.madamandeve.co.za
ZUMA COULDN'T CARE LESS
HEH. HEH. HEH.

AND IN OTHER NEWS, THE **SABC** SAYS THAT, IN ADDITION TO A **TV LICENCE**, USERS SHOULD ALSO PAY FOR A **LAPTOP LICENCE** AND A **CELLPHONE LICENCE**.

WHAT?!

HELLO. HAVE YOU PAID YOUR CARTOON LICENCE YET? PLEASE SEND TWENTY FIVE BUCKS TO THANDI SISULU AT...

SLAM!!

I WAS GONNA GIVE YOU HALF!

Hello. This is the **SABC**. Pay your **TV licence**.

Hello. This is the **SABC**. Pay your **cellphone licence**.

Hello. This is the **SABC**. Pay your **microwave licence**.

Hello. This is the **SABC**...

AND IN OTHER NEWS... PRESIDENT ZUMA SAID HE WILL STOP SPEAKING ANYTIME HE RECEIVES MORE BOOS.

"RECEIVES MORE BOOS."

"RECEIVE MORE BOOS."

"RECEIVE MORE BOOZE."

EVE!! IT'S AFTER FIVE! WHERE'S MY GIN & TONIC?!

MADAM & Eve

BY STEPHEN FRANCIS & RICO

OKAY. FIRST OF ALL... I HAD A DREAM.

...WHICH MATCHED EXACTLY WHAT THE VOICES IN MY HEAD TOLD ME PREVIOUSLY.

THE FOLLOWING DAY... THERE WERE SIGNS I COULDN'T IGNORE.

A TINGLING IN MY FINGERTIPS..., AND STRANGE CLOUD FORMATIONS RESEMBLING MY ENEMIES.

©RAPID PHASE · 2017

I ALSO STEPPED ON CRACKS IN THE SIDEWALK, WHICH WAS EXTREMELY SIGNIFICANT.

THEN, I WAS HANDED A TOP SECRET INTELLIGENCE REPORT WITH EVIDENCE OF TREASONOUS PLOTTING!

WHICH, UNFORTUNATELY, I CAN'T SHOW TO YOU, BECAUSE MY DOG ATE IT!

HEY!!

...AND THAT'S WHY I RESHUFFLED MY CABINET...

... AND FIRED MY TWO MOST SENIOR FINANCIAL OFFICIALS.

HIS DOG ATE HIS INTELLIGENCE REPORT?!

GWEN! GET IN HERE!!

Panel 1: LOOK CLOSELY, MOM. CHECK OUT MY FINGERPRINT. — DON'T TELL ME. TELL EVE.

Panel 2: LOOK CLOSELY, EVE. CHECK OUT MY THUMB PRINT! — DON'T BLAME ME. I JUST DUSTED.

Panel 3: FINE! I UPGRADE TO A NEW SMARTPHONE WITH A FINGERPRINT SCANNER AND NOBODY CARES!

Panel 4: I CARE! CAN I PLAY POKEMON GO?

Panel 5: IT'S AFTER FIVE!! TIME FOR MY GIN & TONIC!! — ARE YOU SURE YOU NEED ONE?

Panel 6: DID I ASK YOU?! MIND YOUR OWN BUSINESS! — FINE!

Panel 7: EXCUSE ME FOR CARING! NEXT TIME, I'LL KEEP QUIET! — GOOD!

Panel 8: HERE'S YOUR DRINK. — THANKS. ...AND TURN OFF SIRI. — SEE IF I CARE.

Panel 9: ATTENTION TEACHERS OF CAPITALIST DOGMA! — GASP!

Panel 10: We have hacked into this computer and KIDNAPPED Thandi's HOMEWORK! If you want to see it again, pay a RANSOM of 300 RUBLES, two Justin Bieber tickets and...

Panel 11: DON'T WORRY... I TOLD THEM WE DON'T NEGOTIATE WITH CYBER TERRORISTS!

Panel 12: "JUSTIN BIEBER TICKETS?" — WHO SAYS THE RUSSIANS AREN'T BELIEBERS?

MADAM & Eve

BY STEPHEN FRANCIS & RICO

ATTENTION IMPERIALIST SOUTH AFRICAN COMPUTER USER! WE ARE **RUSSIAN HACKERS** AND HAVE TAKEN **CONTROL** OF THIS COMPUTER AND **KIDNAPPED** YOUR IMPORTANT FILES!

:GASP!!:

FILES? WHAT IMPORTANT FILES?!

MY GOOGLE MAPS SHOE SALE FILES! MY LIFE IS RUINED!

IF YOU DON'T WANT YOUR LIFE RUINED, YOU MUST MEET OUR DEMANDS!

JA! HERE'S WHERE THEY ASK FOR MONEY!!

WE DON'T WANT YOUR MONEY.

INSTEAD, WE WISH YOU TO CORRECT A TERRIBLE INJUSTICE.

ON BEHALF OF OUR HARD-WORKING COMRADE, EVE SISULU.

FIRST... SHE MUST HAVE A **LARGE WAGE INCREASE.**

NO PROBLEM! JUST GIVE US BACK THOSE SHOE SALE FILES!

SECOND, SHE GETS AT LEAST ONE MORE DAY OFF PER WEEK!

A WHOLE DAY OFF?

...THESE RUSSIANS DRIVE A HARD BARGAIN.

AND LET'S NOT FORGET THANDI SISULU... WHO MAY REQUIRE A DOCTOR'S NOTE CORROBORATING HER ACCOUNT OF A DOG-EATING HOMEWORK INCIDENT FROM TIME TO TIME.

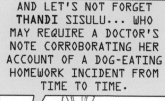

SLAM!!

"...DOG-EATING HOMEWORK INCIDENT?"

IT LOOKED GOOD ON PAPER.

© RAPID PHASE 2017

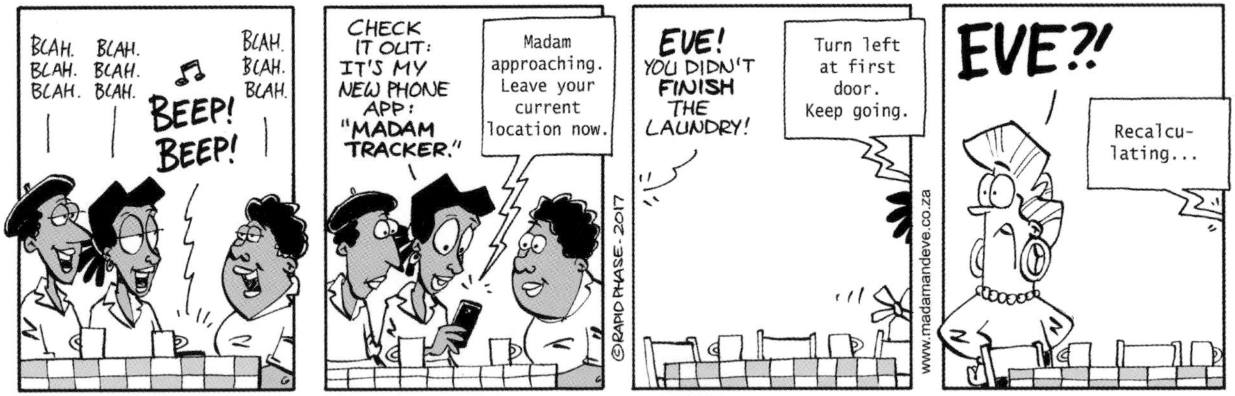
BLAH. BLAH. BLAH.
BLAH. BLAH. BLAH.
BEEP! BEEP!
BLAH. BLAH. BLAH.
CHECK IT OUT: IT'S MY NEW PHONE APP: "MADAM TRACKER."
Madam approaching. Leave your current location now.
©RAPID PHASE·2017
EVE! YOU DIDN'T FINISH THE LAUNDRY!
Turn left at first door. Keep going.
www.madamandeve.co.za
EVE?!
Recalcu-lating...

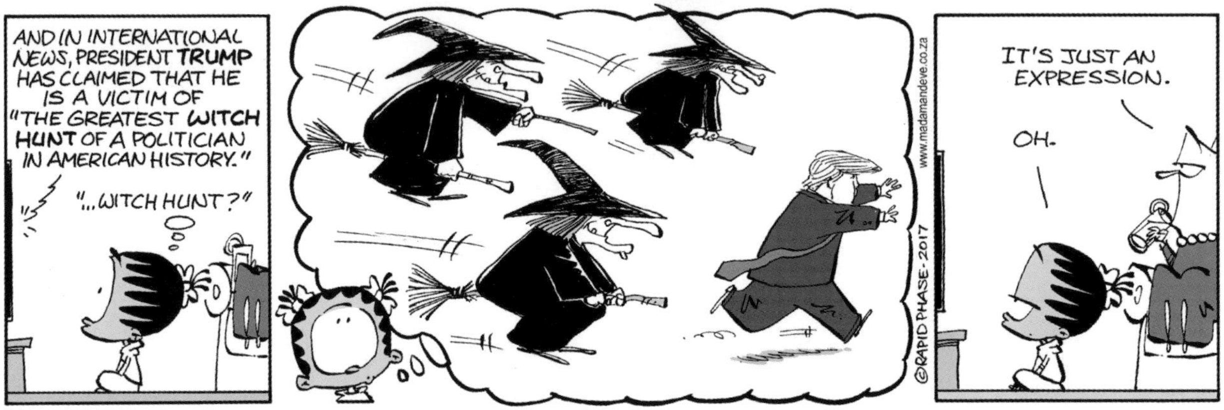
AND IN INTERNATIONAL NEWS, PRESIDENT TRUMP HAS CLAIMED THAT HE IS A VICTIM OF "THE GREATEST WITCH HUNT OF A POLITICIAN IN AMERICAN HISTORY."
"...WITCH HUNT?"
www.madamandeve.co.za
©RAPID PHASE·2017
IT'S JUST AN EXPRESSION.
OH.

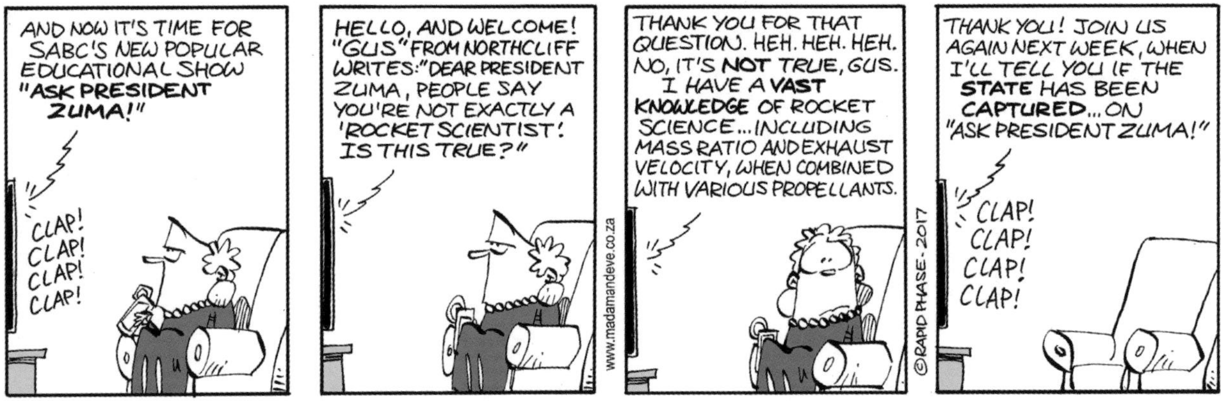
AND NOW IT'S TIME FOR SABC'S NEW POPULAR EDUCATIONAL SHOW "ASK PRESIDENT ZUMA!"
CLAP! CLAP! CLAP! CLAP!
HELLO, AND WELCOME! "GUS" FROM NORTHCLIFF WRITES: "DEAR PRESIDENT ZUMA, PEOPLE SAY YOU'RE NOT EXACTLY A 'ROCKET SCIENTIST'. IS THIS TRUE?"
www.madamandeve.co.za
THANK YOU FOR THAT QUESTION. HEH. HEH. HEH. NO, IT'S NOT TRUE, GUS. I HAVE A VAST KNOWLEDGE OF ROCKET SCIENCE... INCLUDING MASS RATIO AND EXHAUST VELOCITY, WHEN COMBINED WITH VARIOUS PROPELLANTS.
©RAPID PHASE·2017
THANK YOU! JOIN US AGAIN NEXT WEEK, WHEN I'LL TELL YOU IF THE STATE HAS BEEN CAPTURED... ON "ASK PRESIDENT ZUMA!"
CLAP! CLAP! CLAP! CLAP!

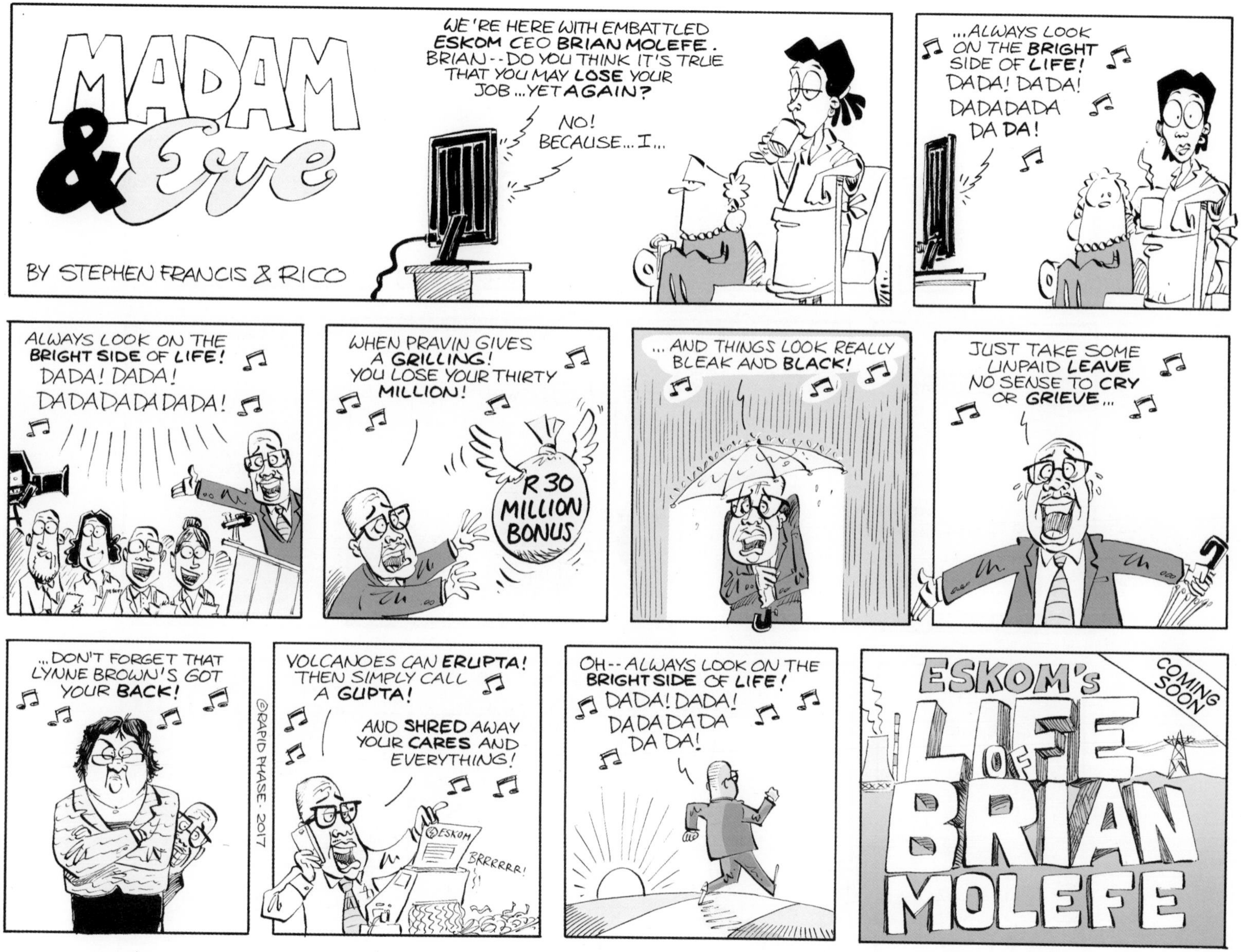
MADAM & Eve
BY STEPHEN FRANCIS & RICO
WE'RE HERE WITH EMBATTLED ESKOM CEO BRIAN MOLEFE. BRIAN--DO YOU THINK IT'S TRUE THAT YOU MAY LOSE YOUR JOB...YET AGAIN?
NO! BECAUSE... I...
...ALWAYS LOOK ON THE BRIGHT SIDE OF LIFE! DADA! DADA! DADADADA DA DA!
ALWAYS LOOK ON THE BRIGHT SIDE OF LIFE! DADA! DADA! DADADADADADA!
WHEN PRAVIN GIVES A GRILLING! YOU LOSE YOUR THIRTY MILLION!
R 30 MILLION BONUS
...AND THINGS LOOK REALLY BLEAK AND BLACK!
JUST TAKE SOME UNPAID LEAVE NO SENSE TO CRY OR GRIEVE...
...DON'T FORGET THAT LYNNE BROWN'S GOT YOUR BACK!
©RAPID PHASE 2017
VOLCANOES CAN ERUPTA! THEN SIMPLY CALL A GUPTA!
AND SHRED AWAY YOUR CARES AND EVERYTHING!
ESKOM
BRRRRRR!
OH--ALWAYS LOOK ON THE BRIGHT SIDE OF LIFE! DADA! DADA! DADADADA DA DA!
ESKOM'S LIFE OF BRIAN MOLEFE
COMING SOON

Panel 1: AND IN OTHER NEWS... THE INVESTIGATION INTO POSSIBLE TIES BETWEEN **RUSSIA** AND **TRUMP** ASSOCIATES ...HAS IDENTIFIED A **WHITE HOUSE OFFICIAL**...

Panel 2:  ...AS A **SIGNIFICANT PERSON** OF **INTEREST.**

Panel 3:  ARE YOU IN TROUBLE FOR NOT HANDING IN YOUR **HOMEWORK?** | LET'S JUST SAY... I'M A "SIGNIFICANT PERSON OF INTEREST."

Panel 4:  ...AND SO IS MY **NEIGHBOUR'S DOG.**

Panel 5:  WHAT ARE YOU BUSY WITH? | A SCHOOL REPORT ON **POLITICAL SCANDALS!**

Panel 6:  IT'S HARD KEEPING TRACK OF ALL THE **GATES.** GUPTA-GATE, NENE-GATE, ESKOM-GATE, SHEBEEN-GATE, HLAUDI-GATE... MOLEFE-GATE...

Panel 7:  YOU WANT A **COOL DRINK?** | GOT ANY **GATE**-ORADE?

Panel 8:  I WAS **SERIOUS!** I LIKE THE STUFF!

Panel 9:  DOES PRESIDENT **ZUMA** GET TO TAKE **PAID LEAVE?**

Panel 10:  THAT'S NOT THE **PROBLEM**...

Panel 11:  THE **PROBLEM** IS GETTING HIM TO LEAVE... **UNPAID.**

Panel 12:  BOOM. MIC DROP! | **MOM!!**

COMMENTATORS ARE SAYING, THAT TIRED OF **PRESIDENT ZUMA** RUNNING THE COUNTRY LIKE A **BANANA REPUBLIC**...

...THE **ANC** HAS NOW OFFICIALLY SPLIT.

IT'S A **BANANA REPUBLIC** SPLIT!!

WANNA GET SOME **ICE CREAM?**

HOW CAN I **TELL** IF I'VE BEEN **CAPTURED?**

DO YOU HAVE THE **GUPTAS** ON **SPEED DIAL?**

NO.

DID SOMEONE GIVE YOU A NEW **LUXURY CAR** AND **HIRE YOUR FAMILY?**

NO!

DID SOMEONE FLY YOU TO **DUBAI FIRST CLASS** AND BUY YOU A **FANCY HOUSE?**

NO!!

THEN **RELAX.** NOTHING TO WORRY ABOUT.

SOMEBODY **CAPTURE** ME!!

DONALD TRUMP... HELEN ZILLE... HLAUDI MOTSOENENG...

...THEY **PROWL** THE EMPTY **TWEETS** AT **NIGHT!**

THESE ARE THE MEN AND WOMEN OF...

TWEET SQUAD! ...COMING SOON TO SABC!

ZZZZZ

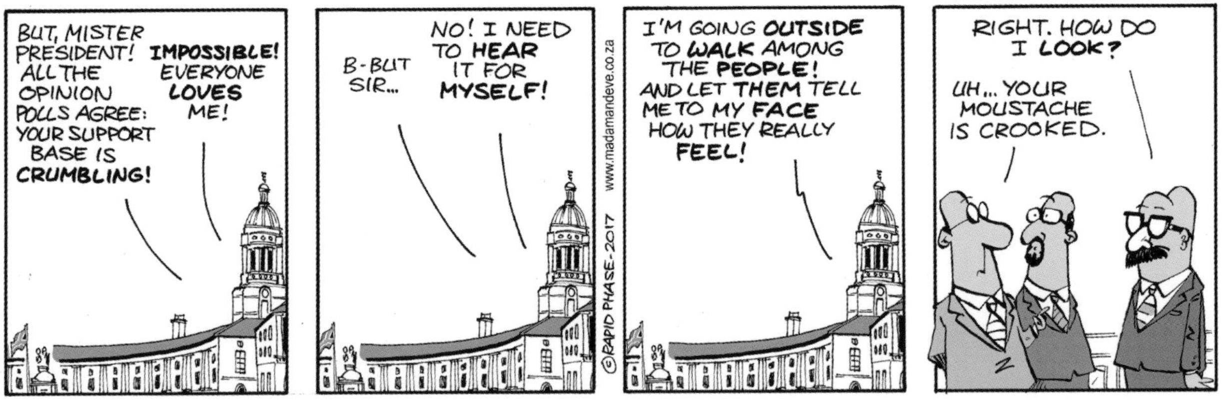
BUT, MISTER PRESIDENT! ALL THE OPINION POLLS AGREE: YOUR SUPPORT BASE IS CRUMBLING!
IMPOSSIBLE! EVERYONE LOVES ME!
B-BUT SIR...
NO! I NEED TO HEAR IT FOR MYSELF!
©RAPID PHASE-2017 www.madamandeve.co.za
I'M GOING OUTSIDE TO WALK AMONG THE PEOPLE! AND LET THEM TELL ME TO MY FACE HOW THEY REALLY FEEL!
RIGHT. HOW DO I LOOK?
UH... YOUR MOUSTACHE IS CROOKED.

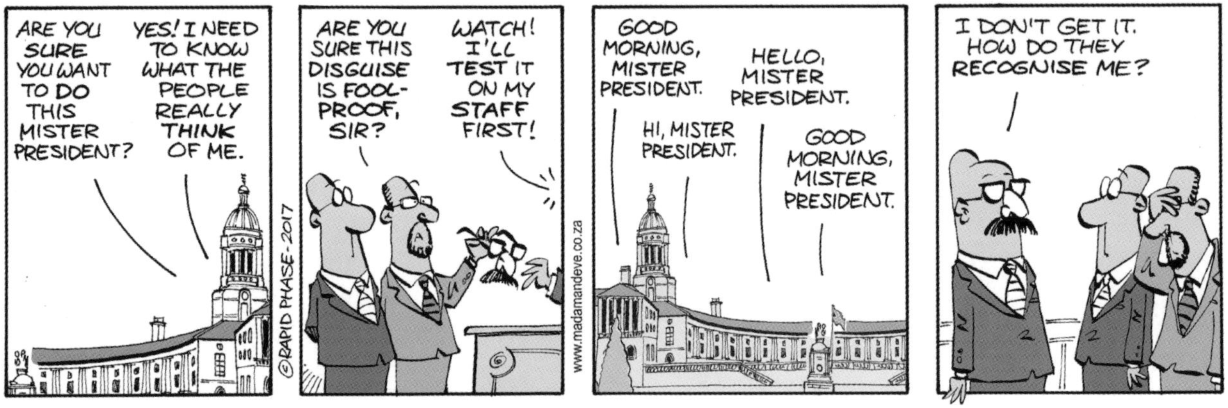
ARE YOU SURE YOU WANT TO DO THIS MISTER PRESIDENT?
YES! I NEED TO KNOW WHAT THE PEOPLE REALLY THINK OF ME.
©RAPID PHASE-2017
ARE YOU SURE THIS DISGUISE IS FOOL-PROOF, SIR?
WATCH! I'LL TEST IT ON MY STAFF FIRST!
www.madamandeve.co.za
GOOD MORNING, MISTER PRESIDENT.
HELLO, MISTER PRESIDENT.
HI, MISTER PRESIDENT.
GOOD MORNING, MISTER PRESIDENT.
I DON'T GET IT. HOW DO THEY RECOGNISE ME?

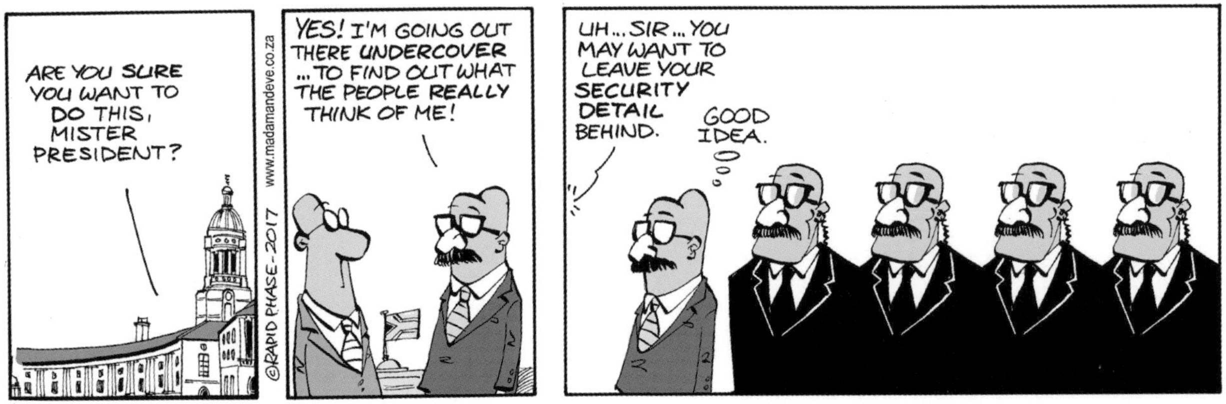
ARE YOU SURE YOU WANT TO DO THIS, MISTER PRESIDENT?
www.madamandeve.co.za ©RAPID PHASE-2017
YES! I'M GOING OUT THERE UNDERCOVER ...TO FIND OUT WHAT THE PEOPLE REALLY THINK OF ME!
UH... SIR... YOU MAY WANT TO LEAVE YOUR SECURITY DETAIL BEHIND.
GOOD IDEA.

MADAM & EVE

BY STEPHEN FRANCIS & RICO

AT LEAST YOU HAVE YOUR **HEALTH.** THANK YOU. **NEXT!**

NO **LOAD SHEDDING** SO FAR THIS YEAR. THANK YOU. **NEXT!**

WELL, THE **RAND** CAN'T GET MUCH **LOWER.** THANK YOU.

NEXT.

GUARANTEED **GOOD NEWS** Only R 20

OKAY-- HERE'S MY TWENTY BUCKS...

...TELL ME SOMETHING **GOOD** ABOUT **ZUMA.**

WHAT HAPPENED?

I GOT A **REFUND.**

©RAPID PHASE-2017

111

HOOT IF YOU STILL LIKE ZUMA!

HOOT! HOOT! HOOT! HOOT!! HOOT! HOOT! HOOT!

THEY LIKE ME! THEY STILL REALLY LIKE ME!

GOOD NEWS

ONLY 10 RAND

OKAY. HERE'S MY TEN BUCKS. WHAT'S THE GOOD NEWS?

THERE ISN'T ANY...

WHAT?! YOU PROMISED ME GOOD NEWS!

I COULD HAVE CHARGED YOU TWENTY.

I CAN'T TAKE IT ANYMORE!

BIG GOLDEN HAND-SHAKES AND PLUGGED LEAKING EMAILS!

DENIALS, REPRISALS AND LARGE NUCLEAR SIDE DEALS! REFUNDS, CORRUPTION... AVOIDING HAWK STINGS!

THESE ARE A FEW OF THEIR FAVOURITE THINGS!

SLAM!!

OH, COME ON! THAT WAS A GOOD ONE!

MADAM & Eve

BY STEPHEN FRANCIS & RICO

AND IN OTHER NEWS, NEWLY RELEASED **LEAKED EMAILS** REVEAL THAT THE **GUPTAS** WERE PLANNING TO **BUY** ONE OF THEIR LEADING CRITICS...

...THE **MAIL & GUARDIAN** NEWSPAPER.

ACCORDING TO REPORTS... AFTER THE **ACQUISITION**, THE **GUPTAS** PLANNED TO **TURN** THE **MAIL & GUARDIAN**...

...INTO A **PUPPET PAPER**.

CRASH!

©RAPD PHASE 2017

ARE YOU OKAY?

RUSSIAN NUCLEAR POWER IS THE WAVE OF THE **FUTURE**. I HOPE THE GOVERNMENT CHOOSES IT!

I WISH PEOPLE WOULD JUST LEAVE PRESIDENT **ZUMA ALONE**! HE'S JUST TRYING TO GIVE US A **BETTER LIFE** FOR ALL!

SEE YOU LATER! EVE AND I ARE GOING TO ANOTHER BIG PROTEST **RALLY**!

HANDS OFF PRESIDENT **ZUMA**!

DOWN WITH WHITE MONOPOLY CAPITAL!

AAAH!!

PUPPETS!! WE'RE BEING TURNED INTO **GUPTA** PUPPETS!!

NO MORE LEFT-OVER **CURRY** FOR LUNCH.

RUB-A-DUB-DUB,
THREE MEN IN A LEAKY TUB,
AND WHO DO YOU THINK
THEY WERE?

THE FIXER, THE FAKER,
THE CROOKED DEAL MAKER,
THE **EMAILS LEAKED** OUT FOR
ALL TO SEE...

S.S. GUPTA

WAIT A MINUTE!! THAT'S **NOT** HOW I REMEMBER IT!!

IT'S THE NEW, UPDATED "STATE CAPTURE" VERSION.

MOM!!

Humpty Molefe sat on a wall,

Humpty Molefe had a great fall.

All the king's ministers and all the board's men Couldn't put Humpty Molefe together again.

LET ME GUESS... IT'S THE NEW, UPDATED "ESKOM" VERSION.

YOU GOT IT IN ONE.

AND SO, THE **FIRST LITTLE PIG'S HOUSE** WAS HUFFED AND PUFFED AND **BLOWN AWAY** BY CAPE **STORMS**...

THE **SECOND LITTLE PIG'S HOUSE** WAS **BURNED** DOWN BY THE KNYSNA **FIRES**...

...AND THE **THIRD** LITTLE PIG'S **BRICK HOUSE** WAS **REPOSSESSED** BY THE **WOLF** (WHO WAS EMPLOYED BY THE BANK) DUE TO THE **RECESSION**.

...**THAT'S** THE STORY OF THE **THREE LITTLE PIGS**?!

UPDATED FOR 2017.

www.madamandeve.co.za

©RAPID PHASE-2017

YOU KEEP STARING AT THAT THING FOR HOURS!

IT'S THE LATEST CRAZE! ...A FIDGET SPINNER!

www.madamandeve.co.za

IT'S MY KEY TO ENTERING THE WORLD OF POLITICS.

©RAPID PHASE-2017

I'M GOING TO BECOME A FIDGET SPIN DOCTOR!

SHE KICKED YOU OUTSIDE?

AM I OUTSIDE?

THE STAGES OF HLAUDI GRIEF:

① DENIAL

HLAUDI IS FIRED FROM THE SABC? IMPOSSIBLE!

② ANGER AND BARGAINING

NOBODY FIRES HLAUDI!

BOFF!

©RAPID PHASE-2017

www.madamandeve.co.za

③ ACCEPTANCE

I...I GUESS IT'S TRUE... HLAUDI IS FIRED.

④ CALL A FRIEND

HELP!

You've reached Jacob Zuma. I can't take your call right now. Please leave a message after...

AND NOW FOR THE SABC WEATHER REPORT...

©RAPID PHASE-2017

HLAUDI...

www.madamandeve.co.za

...WITH A 90% CHANCE OF SHOWERS.

HLAUDI IS FIRED!! BWAWAAA!!

MADAM & EVE'S
WHEN **NOT** TO USE AN **UBER** IN SOUTH AFRICA.

QUICK! WHERE'S OUR **GETAWAY** CAR?!

IT'S OKAY! "FRED, OUR **UBER** DRIVER WILL BE HERE IN TWO MINUTES."

RADICAL ECONOMIC TRANSFORMATION

Only 20 Rand

OKAY. HERE'S MY **MONEY.** WHAT HAPPENS **NOW?**

NOTHING! I JUST RADICALLY **TRANSFORMED** YOUR ECONOMIC SITUATION BY **MINUS** TWENTY BUCKS.

IT'S OKAY-- EVEN **PRAVIN** ISN'T SURE HOW TO DEFINE RADICAL ECONOMIC TRANSFORMATION.

HELP REDISTRIBUTE WHITE MONOPOLY CAPITAL

Only 20 Rand

YOU THINK I'M **STUPID?** YOU'LL TAKE MY **TWENTY** BUCKS AND THANK ME FOR "REDISTRIBUTING MY CAPITAL."

OKAY. I'LL GIVE YOU A **DISCOUNT**-- FOR **YOU,** ONLY **TEN** BUCKS!

THAT'S MORE **LIKE** IT!

MADAM & Eve

BY STEPHEN FRANCIS & RICO

READY?

READY.

CHING! CHONG! CHA!

YES! ROCK BEATS SCISSORS! I WIN!!

NOT SO FAST. BEST TWO OUT OF THREE.

SIGH.

CHING...CHONG...CHA!!

YES! SCISSORS CUT PAPER! I WIN!!

NOT SO FAST, BEST THREE OUT OF FIVE.

CHING...CHONG...CHA!

YES! I WIN AGAIN!!

BEST FIVE OUT OF SEVEN.

ANNUAL WAGE NEGOTIATIONS?

YOU GOT IT.

RIGHT! BEST OUT OF 45!

SIGH.

© RAPID PHASE - 2017

COMING UP... OUR **INVESTIGATION** INTO SOUTH AFRICA'S **NEWEST** THREAT!

...**BEYOND** RADICAL ECONOMIC TRANSFORMATION!

...**WORSE** THAN WHITE MONOPOLY CAPITAL! IT'S --

...WHITE MONOPOLY RADICAL ECONOMIC CAPITAL TRANSFORMATION!

GWEN!!

AND, IN OTHER NEWS... AFTER QUESTIONING IN PARLIAMENT, PRESIDENT **ZUMA** SAID "SOUTH AFRICA IS **RUNNING WELL** UNDER HIM."

OINK! OINK! OINK!

FLAP! FLAP! FLAP!

MOTHER ANDERSON'S EXOTIC SOUTH AFRICAN COCKTAILS

LEAKY GUPTA
CAPTURE ONE SHOT VODKA. CAPTURE A DASH OF CURRY. TOMATO JUICE, PUNCH HOLE IN BOTTOM OF GLASS.

TWEETY ZILLE
ONE SHOT WHITE RUM, ONE SHOT DARK RUM, KEEP SEPARATE, PUT ON ICE AND CHILL. PROMISE TO STOP TWEETING.

JUNK STATUS
BITTER LEMON, TWO SHOTS TEQUILA, SLICE OF LEMON, LOTS OF BITTERS, MORE BITTERS. DOWN IN ONE AND THEN RESHUFFLE YOUR CABINET.

MADAM & Eve

BY STEPHEN FRANCIS & RICO

COFFEE?
...EVE AND I ARE TRADING PLACES FOR THE DAY TO SEE WHOSE LIFE IS MORE DEMANDING.

HOW HARD CAN IT BE?

WHEN'S THE FIRST SOAP OPERA ON?

VRR RRR

DON'T FORGET TO DRY THEM.

OH. LOOK! A SHOE SALE!

EVE!!...I MEAN GWEN! IT'S AFTER FIVE! WHERE'S MY GIN & TONIC?!

©RAPID PHASE - 2017

SO. HOW WAS YOUR DAY?

P-PASS ME THAT NEWSPAPER.

NEWS

ZZZZZ

Row 1:

THANDI! WHERE'S YOUR...

"THANDI?!"

...I AM WONDER WOMAN!

WONDER WOMAN DOES NOT NEED TO **WORRY** ABOUT "PALTRY" **HOMEWORK!!**

"WONDER WOMAN" GOT SENT TO THE PRINCIPAL'S OFFICE.

OH, SHUT UP.

PRINCIP

Row 2:

COMING UP... EYEWITNESS **FAKE NEWS!**

...FOLLOWED BY **FAKE WEATHER** AND **FAKE SPORT.**

BUT FIRST, A WORD FROM OUR **FAKE** SPONSOR.

...YOU'RE WATCHING THE **REALITY CHANNEL.**

Row 3:

LOOK AT ZUMA'S **HEAD.** IT'S **IRREGULAR.**

JA.

WHAT DO YOU THINK **HAPPENED?**

I HEARD THAT SOME **MP'S** HIT HIM WITH WHAT HE'S MOST **AFRAID OF.**

...A **SECRET MALLET.**

TWO THINGS THAT MAY BE FOUND IN THE PRESIDENT'S POCKET

POCKET PROTECTOR

PUBLIC PROTECTOR

BIRD FLU OUTBREAK IN SOUTH AFRICA

BLESS YOU.

SNIFF!

IN TODAY'S HEADLINES... EMAIL LEAKS REVEAL THAT **R 30 MILLION** OF **TAXPAYERS'** MONEY WAS FRAUDULENTLY USED TO **PAY** FOR THE 2013 **GUPTA WEDDING**...

TAXPAYERS ARE ALSO FUNDING A **R 2.9 BILLION BAILOUT** FOR LOSS–MAKING **SOUTH AFRICAN AIRWAYS**...

BUT FIRST A MESSAGE FROM **SARS**: IT'S **TAX SEASON 2017!** PAY YOUR TAXES!

@#☆%!!!

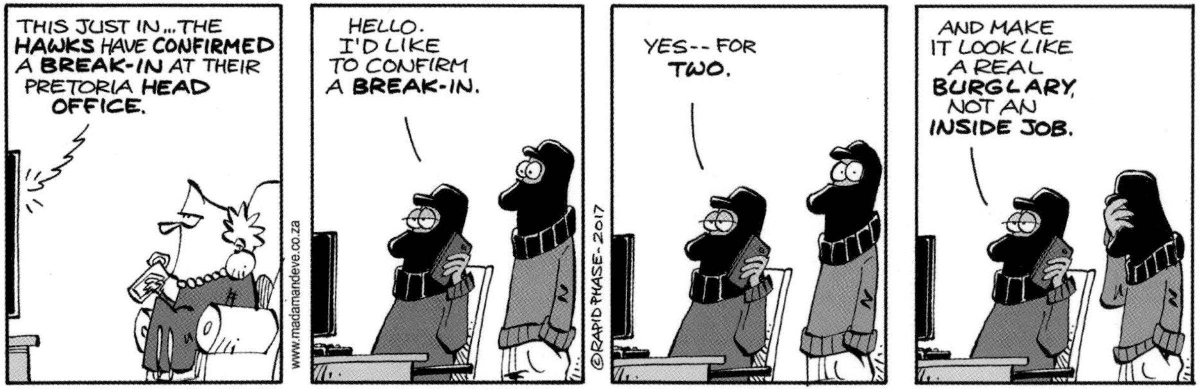
THIS JUST IN... THE HAWKS HAVE CONFIRMED A BREAK-IN AT THEIR PRETORIA HEAD OFFICE.
www.madamandeve.co.za
HELLO. I'D LIKE TO CONFIRM A BREAK-IN.
©RAPID PHASE-2017
YES-- FOR TWO.
AND MAKE IT LOOK LIKE A REAL BURGLARY, NOT AN INSIDE JOB.

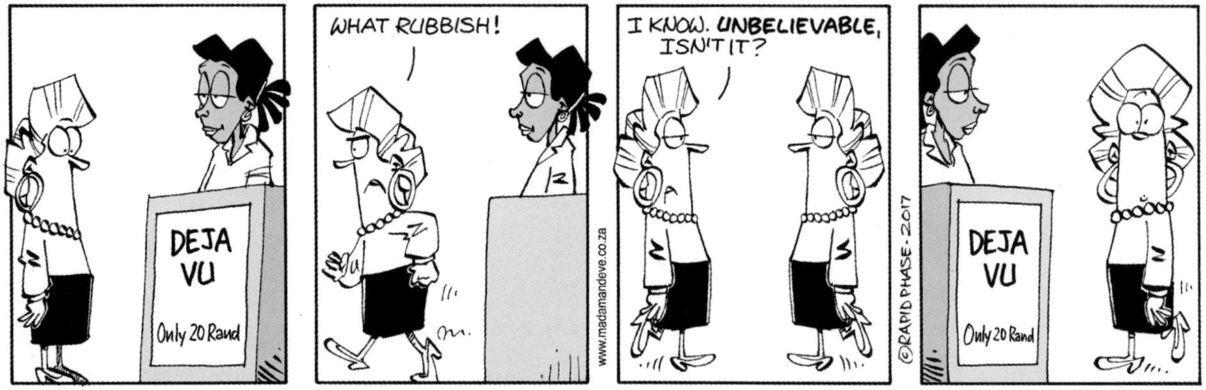
DEJA VU
Only 20 Rand
WHAT RUBBISH!
www.madamandeve.co.za
I KNOW. UNBELIEVABLE, ISN'T IT?
©RAPID PHASE-2017
DEJA VU
Only 20 Rand

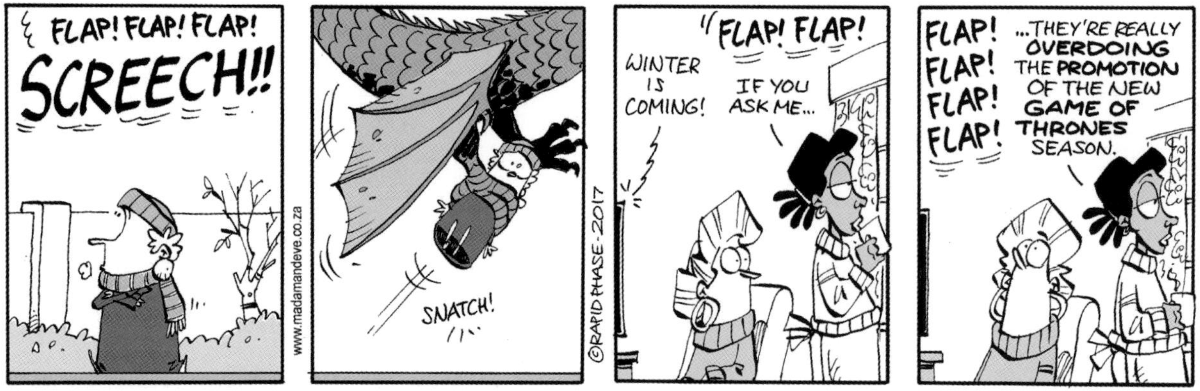
FLAP! FLAP! FLAP!
SCREECH!!
www.madamandeve.co.za
SNATCH!
©RAPID PHASE-2017
FLAP! FLAP!
WINTER IS COMING!
IF YOU ASK ME...
FLAP! FLAP! FLAP! FLAP!
...THEY'RE REALLY OVERDOING THE PROMOTION OF THE NEW GAME OF THRONES SEASON.

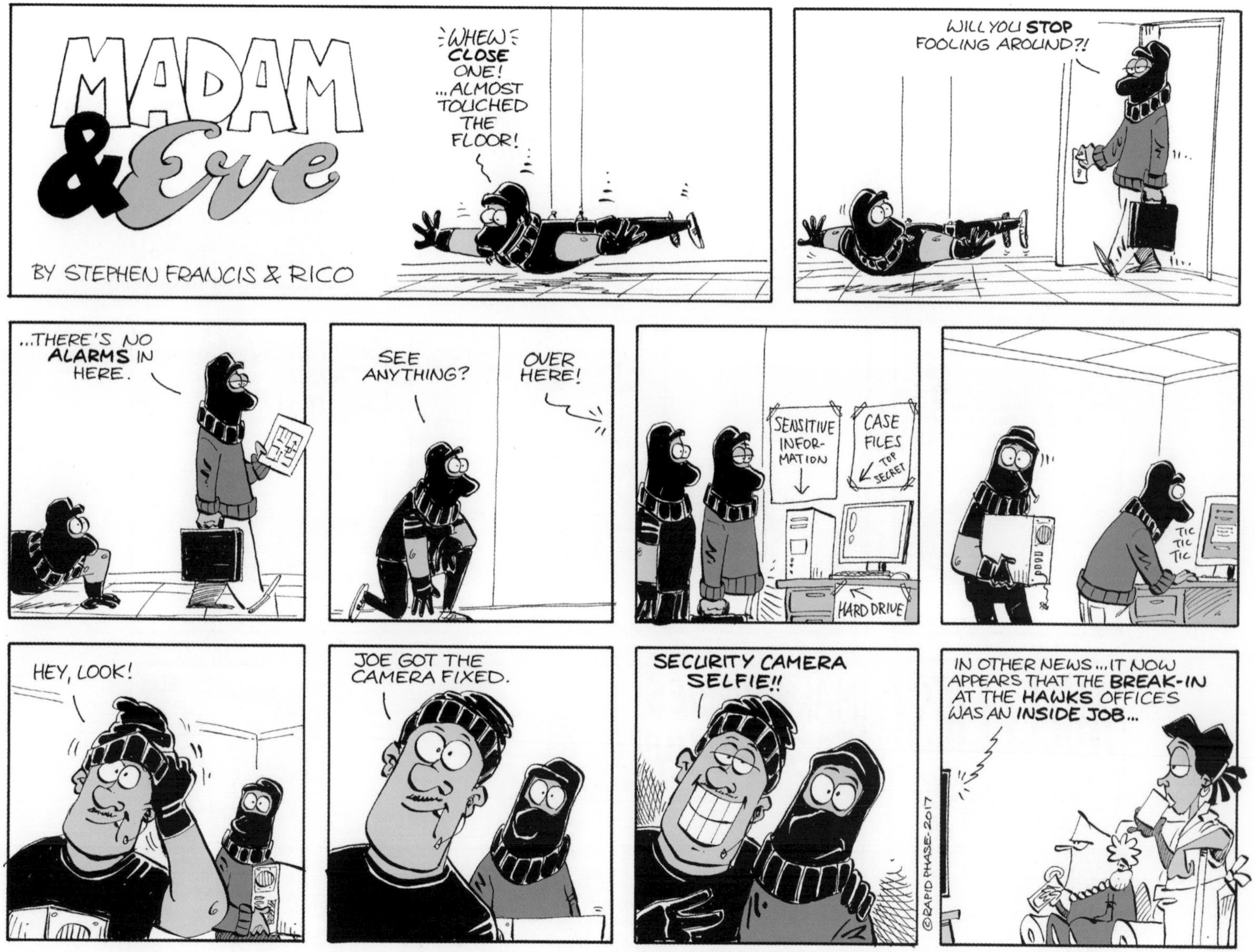
MADAM & Eve
BY STEPHEN FRANCIS & RICO
WHEW CLOSE ONE! ...ALMOST TOUCHED THE FLOOR!
WILL YOU STOP FOOLING AROUND?!
...THERE'S NO ALARMS IN HERE.
SEE ANYTHING?
OVER HERE!
SENSITIVE INFORMATION
CASE FILES
TOP SECRET
HARD DRIVE
TIC TIC TIC
HEY, LOOK!
JOE GOT THE CAMERA FIXED.
SECURITY CAMERA SELFIE!!
©RAPID PHASE 2017
IN OTHER NEWS... IT NOW APPEARS THAT THE BREAK-IN AT THE HAWKS OFFICES WAS AN INSIDE JOB...

OH, NO!! NOT ANOTHER CORRUPTION HEADLINE!!

IN THESE TURBULENT AND STRESSFUL TIMES, WHEN STATE CAPTURE IS EXTENSIVE... AND CORRUPTION IS EVERYWHERE...

WHEN THE PUBLIC PROTECTOR SEEMS USELESS... IT'S TIME FOR A NEW CHAPTER NINE INSTITUTION.

@RAPID PHASE · 2017   www.madamandeve.co.za

THE OFFICE OF THE
PUBLIC PROZACTOR

SHE'LL MAKE YOU FEEL BETTER WHEN TODAY'S HEADLINES GET TOO DEPRESSING.

AND IN OTHER NEWS... SEVEN OPPOSITION PARTIES ARE CALLING ON THE NATIONAL ASSEMBLY SPEAKER TO **RECUSE** HERSELF FROM THE SECRET BALLOT DEBATE.

©RAPID PHASE · 2014   www.madamandeve.co.za

THANDI? WHERE'S TODAY'S **HOMEWORK**?

RIGHT. I HEREBY **RECUSE** MY--

DON'T EVEN THINK ABOUT IT!!

SIGH MONDAYS.

PRINCIPAL

MIELLLIES!

© RAPID PHASE · 2017

MAKE MIELIES GREAT AGAIN!

www.madamandeve.co.za

IN CASE OF EMERGENCY BREAK GLASS

124

MADAM & Eve

BY STEPHEN FRANCIS & RICO

MISTER PRESIDENT, **BELL POTTINGER** ON LINE 2.

≤SIGH≤

...TELL THEM THE **CHEQUE'S** IN THE POST.

MISTER PRESIDENT! WHAT DO YOU **THINK** OF THE **BELL POTTINGER** SCANDAL?!

I HAVE A **PREPARED** STATEMENT.

≤AHEM≤ WHEN IT COMES TO **STIRRING UP** RACIAL TENSIONS... AND SOWING **DIVISIONS**...

WHEN IT COMES TO CYBER-BULLYING, **SPYING** AND SPREADING **FAKE** NEWS...

...OR **PROMOTING** CONFUSING **PHRASEOLOGY** LIKE "WHITE MONOPOLY CAPITAL" ...OR "RADICAL ECONOMIC TRANSFORMATION"..

...OR CONCOCTING PARANOID **"REGIME CHANGE"** CONSPIRACY NARRATIVES...

...WE DON'T NEED SOME **WESTERN** PUBLIC RELATIONS FIRM LIKE **BELL POTTINGER**!

©RAPID PHASE- 2017

...THE **ANC** IS PERFECTLY **CAPABLE** OF DOING ALL THAT BY **THEMSELVES**!

www.madamandeve.co.za

...WHAT?! **HEY!** THAT'S MY **SPEECH!**

MISSING
HAVE YOU SEEN THIS MAN?
SHAUN ABRAHAMS

EVE! IT'S AFTER FIVE! TIME FOR MY GIN & TONIC!!

EVE'S NOT HERE, MOM -- SHE'S TAKEN THE DAY OFF!

IN CASE OF EMERGENCY BREAK GLASS

MADAM & EVE's
GUIDE TO FLIGHTLESS BIRDS OF SOUTHERN AFRICA

OSTRICH

AFRICAN PENGUIN

GUINEAFOWL

SQUAWK!

"CAPTURED" HAWK

MADAM & Eve

BY STEPHEN FRANCIS & RICO

WHAT DOES SHAUN ABRAHAMS DO ALL DAY?

(SINCE HE'S NOT PROSECUTING THE ZUPTAS)

OFFICE WASTEPAPER BASKETBALL

HE SHOOTS! HE **SCORES**!

FUNNY CAT VIDEOS

AG, SHAME! **CUTE**!

MEOW!!

PUTTING PRACTICE

HOLE IN ONE!

GOING OUT FOR COFFEE

I'LL HAVE A SKINNY DOUBLE-SHOT ESPRESSO DECAF MOCHACCINO!

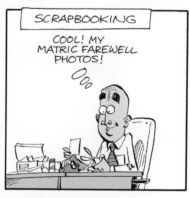

SCRAPBOOKING

COOL! MY MATRIC FAREWELL PHOTOS!

GOING OUT FOR COFFEE

NOT **THIS** GUY AGAIN.

CANDY CRUSH

HOLD ALL MY **CALLS**! I'M IN THE MIDDLE OF SOMETHING IMPORTANT!

Tic Tic Tic Tic Tic Tic

INTERNET CELEBRITY GOSSIP

JAY Z DID **WHAT**?!

BINGE-WATCHING EVERY EPISODE OF "FRIENDS" WITH THE PUBLIC PROTECTOR

ISN'T **JOEY** THE FUNNIEST? I **LOVE** THIS SHOW!!

ZZZZZ

www.madamandeve.co.za

©RAPID PHASE-2017

COME. COME. COME.

COME. COME... STOP! NOW **SIT!!**

GOOD. HOW ABOUT A **TIP?** ... AND I'LL **WATCH** YOUR **CHAIR** WHILE YOU'RE GONE.

SLAM!!
NOBODY APPRECIATES **ENTREPRENEURIAL SPIRIT** THESE DAYS!

©RAPID PHASE · 2017
www.madamandeve.co.za

THANDI! WHERE'S YOUR **HOMEWORK?**
IT'S... A **WORK IN PROGRESS.**

YOU HAVEN'T HANDED IN HOMEWORK FOR THREE WEEKS!!
I **KNOW** THAT!

...DO YOU WANT IT **FAST**, OR DO YOU WANT IT **GOOD?!**

I **THINK** SHE JUST WANTS IT **FINISHED.**
CAN I HELP IT IF I'M A **PERFECTIONIST?**

©RAPID PHASE · 2017
www.madamandeve.co.za

YES, MISTER PRESIDENT?
I JUST HEARD THAT **TRUMP** MAY PARDON HIMSELF.

WHY CAN'T **I** PARDON **MYSELF?**
BUT, SIR-- YOU HAVE **783** CHARGES OF CORRUPTION PENDING.

SO? I'LL JUST PARDON MYSELF SEVEN... ELEVENTY... EIGHT TIMES... UH...

NO. WAIT. SEVEN AND EIGHT ELEVENTY... WAIT. I'LL PARDON MYSELF... DON'T TELL ME...
IS IT LUNCH YET?

©RAPID PHASE · 2017
www.madamandeve.co.za

TRUMP'S NEW WHITE HOUSE SPOKESMAN IS CALLED **SCARAMUCCI.**

SCARAMUCCI?

SCARAMUCCI.

WILL HE DO THE FANDANGO?

THUNDER-BOLTS AND LIGHTNING...

VERY, VERY FRIGHTENING!

GROWNUPS ARE SO **STRANGE** SOMETIMES...

...GALILEO. GALILEO FIGARO!!

DON'T MISS TONIGHT'S SPECIAL REPORT...

..."ARE WE BECOMING TOO **DESENSITISED** TO CORRUPTION?"

UP NEXT...
"THE **BOLD** AND THE **BRIBABLE**"...
"**DAYS** OF OUR **GOLDEN HANDSHAKES**"...
"**BUY** MY **FAMILY**"... AND
"PROJECT **RUNAWAY** (TO **DUBAI**)"...

...YOU'RE WATCHING THE **CORRUPTION** CHANNEL.

GWEN!!

UP NEXT... A GREAT **NEW SHOW** THAT COMBINES **FOOD** PREPARATION **AND** ACCOUNTING!

WE CALL IT:
..."**COOKING THE BOOKS!**"

...YOU'RE WATCHING THE **CORRUPTION** CHANNEL.

...WE'LL BE RIGHT BACK AFTER A WORD FROM OUR **CAPTURER!**

GWEN!!

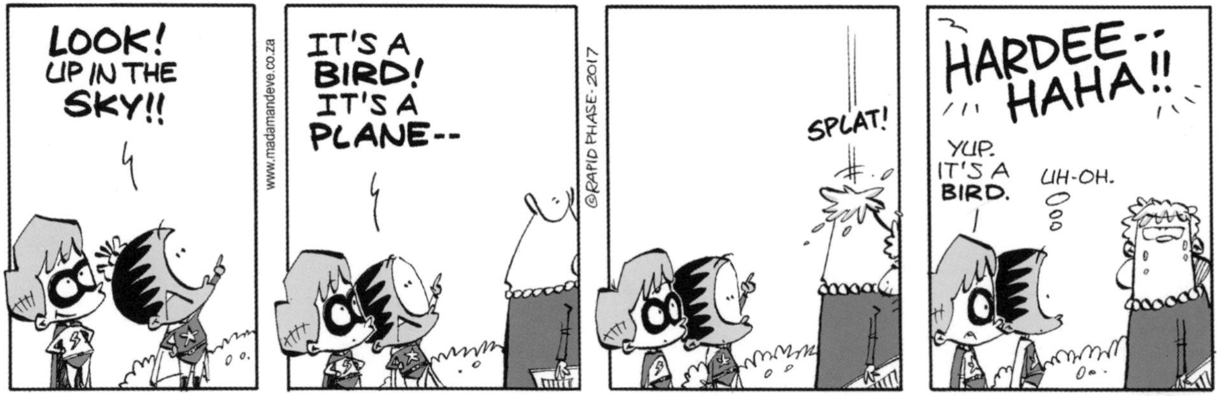
LOOK! UP IN THE SKY!!
www.madamandeve.co.za
IT'S A BIRD! IT'S A PLANE--
©RAPID PHASE 2017
SPLAT!
HARDEE--HAHA!!
YUP. IT'S A BIRD.
UH-OH.

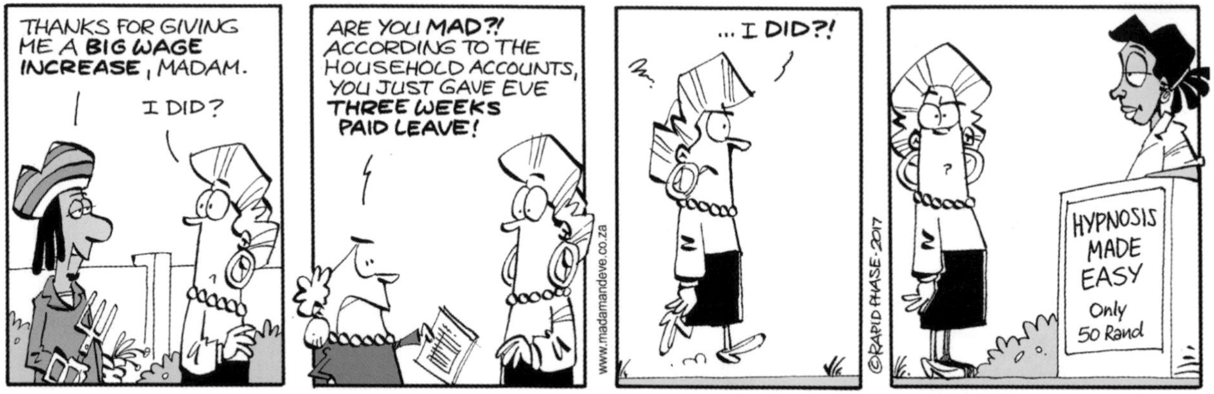
THANKS FOR GIVING ME A BIG WAGE INCREASE, MADAM.
I DID?
ARE YOU MAD?! ACCORDING TO THE HOUSEHOLD ACCOUNTS, YOU JUST GAVE EVE THREE WEEKS PAID LEAVE!
www.madamandeve.co.za
...I DID?!
©RAPID PHASE 2017
HYPNOSIS MADE EASY
Only 50 Rand

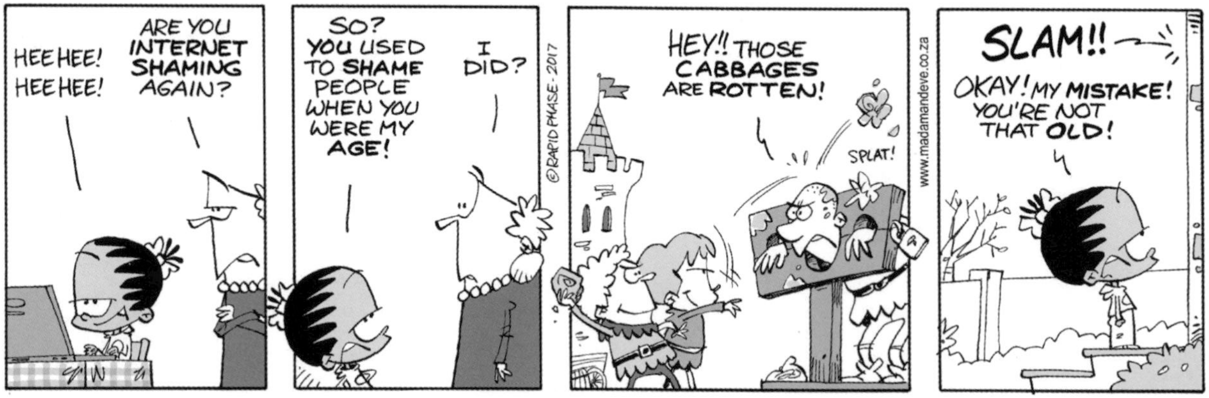
HEE HEE! HEE HEE!
ARE YOU INTERNET SHAMING AGAIN?
SO? YOU USED TO SHAME PEOPLE WHEN YOU WERE MY AGE!
I DID?
©RAPID PHASE 2017
HEY!! THOSE CABBAGES ARE ROTTEN!
SPLAT!
www.madamandeve.co.za
SLAM!!
OKAY! MY MISTAKE! YOU'RE NOT THAT OLD!

MADAM & Eve

BY STEPHEN FRANCIS & RICO

CAN I ASK YOU A QUESTION? WHAT'S A GOLDEN...

UH-OH.

...HANDSHAKE? ⸘WHEW.⸘

IT'S WHEN YOU DID A REALLY BAD JOB AT WORK AND THEY PAY YOU MILLIONS TO STAY HOME AND DO NOTHING.

NO. SERIOUSLY. WHAT'S A "GOLDEN HANDSHAKE?"

I JUST TOLD YOU.

THAT'S SO UNFAIR!! **I KNOW.**

I OFTEN DO A BAD JOB AT SCHOOL AND NOBODY PAYS ME ANYTHING!

STILL... THIS "GOLDEN HANDSHAKE" THING SOUNDS LIKE A SMART CAREER CHOICE.

I'LL CONTINUE DOING BADLY AT SCHOOL AND CONSIDER IT PREPARATION FOR THE FUTURE. **VERY WISE.**

© RAPID PHASE - 2017

EGOLI: PLACE OF GOLDEN HANDSHAKES!

THANKS FOR THE ADVICE. IT'S GOOD TO HAVE GOALS AND ASPIRATIONS. **YOU'RE WELCOME. NOW GO PLAY.**

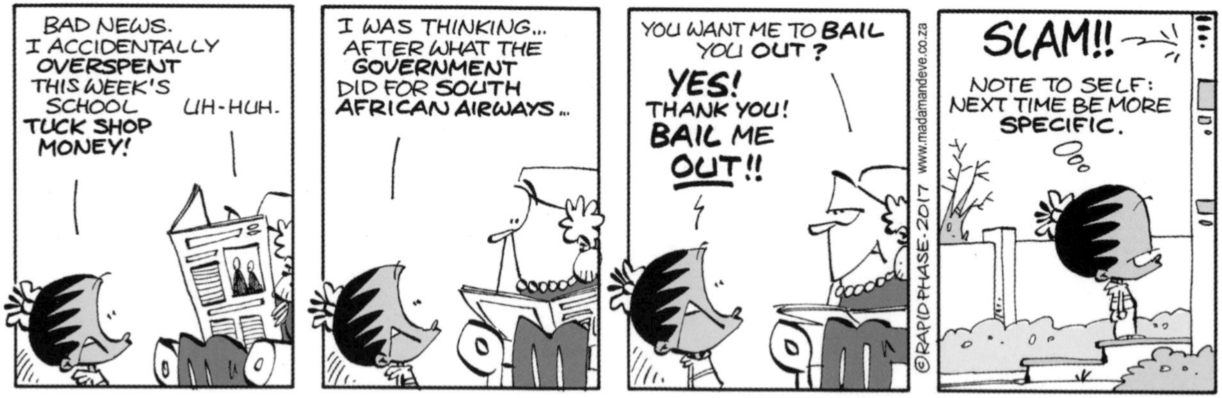
BAD NEWS. I ACCIDENTALLY OVERSPENT THIS WEEK'S SCHOOL TUCK SHOP MONEY!
UH-HUH.
I WAS THINKING... AFTER WHAT THE GOVERNMENT DID FOR SOUTH AFRICAN AIRWAYS...
YOU WANT ME TO BAIL YOU OUT?
YES! THANK YOU! BAIL ME OUT!!
©RAPID PHASE-2017 www.madamandeve.co.za
SLAM!!
NOTE TO SELF: NEXT TIME BE MORE SPECIFIC.

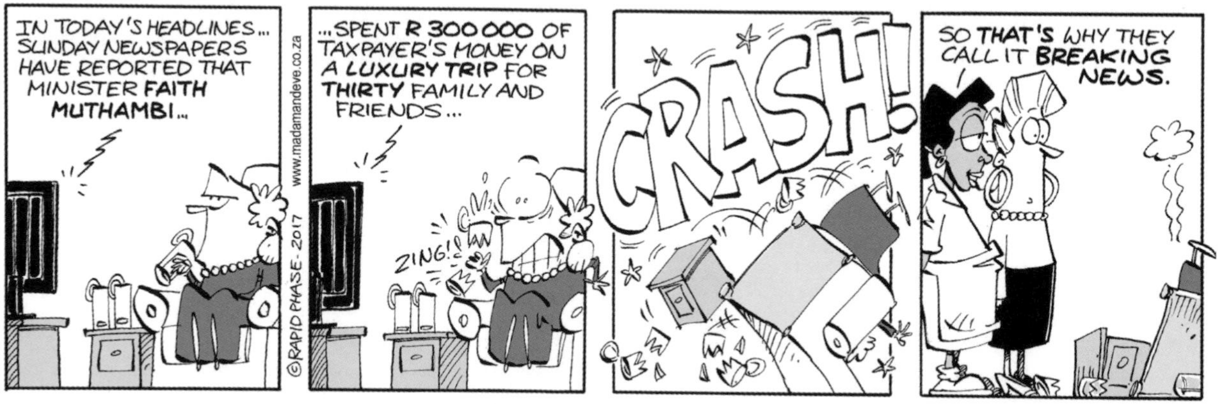
IN TODAY'S HEADLINES... SUNDAY NEWSPAPERS HAVE REPORTED THAT MINISTER FAITH MUTHAMBI...
©RAPID PHASE-2017 www.madamandeve.co.za
...SPENT R 300 000 OF TAXPAYER'S MONEY ON A LUXURY TRIP FOR THIRTY FAMILY AND FRIENDS...
ZING!!
CRASH!
SO THAT'S WHY THEY CALL IT BREAKING NEWS.

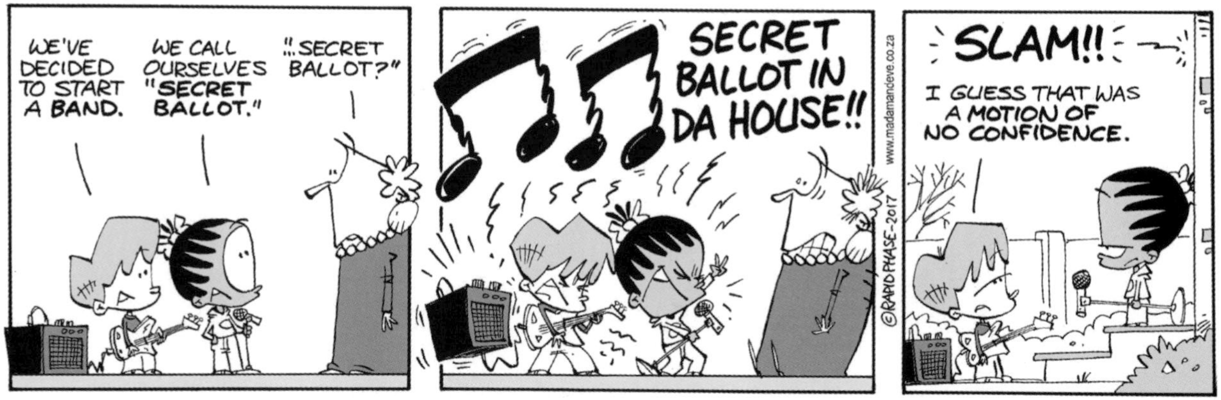
WE'VE DECIDED TO START A BAND.
WE CALL OURSELVES "SECRET BALLOT."
!.. SECRET BALLOT?"
SECRET BALLOT IN DA HOUSE!!
©RAPID PHASE-2017 www.madamandeve.co.za
SLAM!!
I GUESS THAT WAS A MOTION OF NO CONFIDENCE.

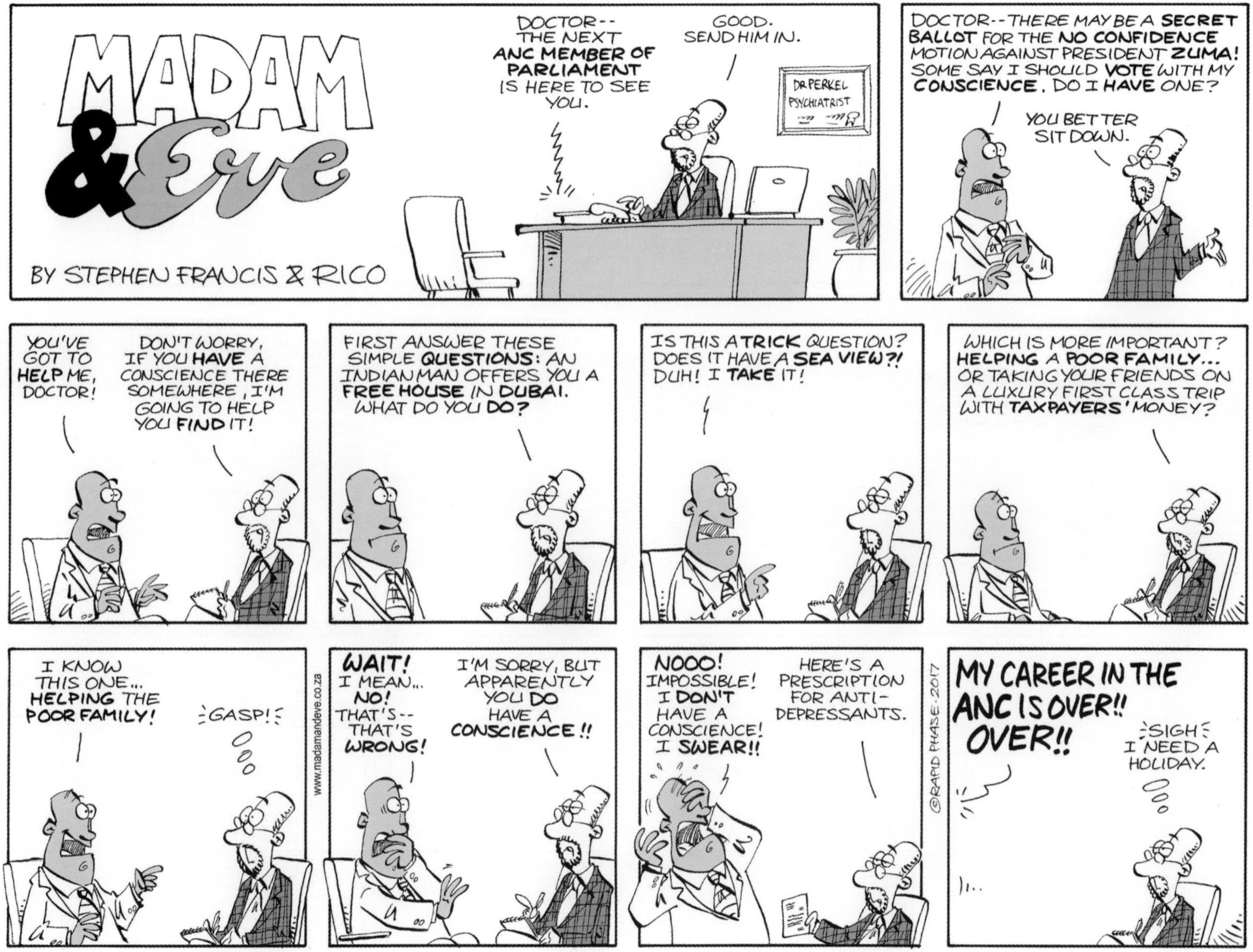
MADAM & Eve
BY STEPHEN FRANCIS & RICO
DOCTOR-- THE NEXT ANC MEMBER OF PARLIAMENT IS HERE TO SEE YOU.
GOOD. SEND HIM IN.
DR PERKEL PSYCHIATRIST
DOCTOR--THERE MAY BE A SECRET BALLOT FOR THE NO CONFIDENCE MOTION AGAINST PRESIDENT ZUMA! SOME SAY I SHOULD VOTE WITH MY CONSCIENCE. DO I HAVE ONE?
YOU BETTER SIT DOWN.
YOU'VE GOT TO HELP ME, DOCTOR!
DON'T WORRY, IF YOU HAVE A CONSCIENCE THERE SOMEWHERE, I'M GOING TO HELP YOU FIND IT!
FIRST ANSWER THESE SIMPLE QUESTIONS: AN INDIAN MAN OFFERS YOU A FREE HOUSE IN DUBAI. WHAT DO YOU DO?
IS THIS A TRICK QUESTION? DOES IT HAVE A SEA VIEW?! DUH! I TAKE IT!
WHICH IS MORE IMPORTANT? HELPING A POOR FAMILY... OR TAKING YOUR FRIENDS ON A LUXURY FIRST CLASS TRIP WITH TAXPAYERS' MONEY?
I KNOW THIS ONE... HELPING THE POOR FAMILY!
GASP!
www.madamandeve.co.za
WAIT! I MEAN... NO! THAT'S-- THAT'S WRONG!
I'M SORRY, BUT APPARENTLY YOU DO HAVE A CONSCIENCE!!
NOOO! IMPOSSIBLE! I DON'T HAVE A CONSCIENCE! I SWEAR!!
HERE'S A PRESCRIPTION FOR ANTI-DEPRESSANTS.
©RAPID PHASE · 2017
MY CAREER IN THE ANC IS OVER!! OVER!!
SIGH I NEED A HOLIDAY.

I'M VERY CONCERNED ABOUT **STATE** CAPTURE.

JOIN THE CLUB.

DESPITE OVERWHELMING **EVIDENCE**, POLICE INTELLIGENCE, THE S.SA, HAWKS, SIU, NPA, THE ANC INTEGRITY COMMISSION, PARLIAMENT...

THE PUBLIC PROSECUTOR AND THE PUBLIC PROTECTOR HAVE DONE **NOTHING** ABOUT **INVESTIGATING** THE **GUPTAS**!

WHO ELSE **IS** THERE?

10:45 AM: I DECIDE TO TAKE THE CASE -- THANDI SISULU, PRIVATE DETECTIVE...

GET YOUR FEET OFF THE FURNITURE!

MY NAME IS SISULU... THANDI SISULU.

MY LINE OF WORK? I'M A **PRIVATE EYE**.

I TAKE MY **JOB** LIKE I TAKE MY **EGGS**.

...HARD-BOILED.

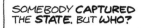

SOMEBODY **CAPTURED** THE **STATE**. BUT **WHO?** NOBODY'S **TALKING**.

...**OR** INVESTIGATING.

SAXONWOLD

THEN A **DAME** WALKS INTO MY OFFICE... WITH AN ENGLISH ACCENT... SAID HER **NAME** WAS **BELLE**...

...**BELLE POTTINGER**.

THANDI SISULU, PRIVATE EYE.

I'M ON THE CLOCK.

SOMEBODY **CAPTURED** THE **STATE**. BUT **WHO?**

THE **GUPTAS**? ...THE **ZUPTAS**?

SAXONWOLD

ALL I NEEDED WAS A **CLUE**.

I KNOW! IT WAS PROFESSOR PLUM AT THE **ABSA** BANK WITH THE **WHITE MONOPOLY CAPITAL**!

THAT WAS PRESIDENT **ZUMA**... HIS STORY HAD MORE **HOLES** THAN A PIECE OF **CHEESE** AT AN **EMMENTAL** CONVENTION.

TO BE CONTINUED...

Panel 1: THANDI SISULU, PRIVATE EYE: THE CASE OF THE **CAPTURED STATE**.

12:45... I GET A **TIP**. SOMEBODY WANTS ME **OFF** THIS CASE... **BADLY**.

©RAPID PHASE 2017

Panel 2: I DECIDE TO "TEST THE WATER..."

≥AHEM≤ I'M SOOO **THIRSTY**! I COULD USE A **COOL DRINK**!

Panel 3: DO THEY THINK I CAN BE **BOUGHT** SO EASILY?

PLOP!

CABINET MINISTER POST

www.madamandeve.co.za

Panel 4: UH-OH.

SIX MONTHS FREE HOMEWORK

Panel 5: HOW'S THE **STATE CAPTURE** INVESTIGATION GOING?

I'M **OFF** THE CASE.

Panel 6: SO. THEY FINALLY **GOT** TO YOU TOO.

HEY! I'M A MEMBER OF **CORRUPTION WATCH**!

©RAPID PHASE. 2017

Panel 7: WHAT'S "CORRUPTION WATCH?"

I PROMISED TO LOOK THE OTHER WAY, AND THEY GAVE ME A NICE **WATCH**.

Panel 8: YOU SHOULD HAVE HELD OUT FOR A **HOUSE** IN **DUBAI**.

IT'S A JOKE! I WAS **JOKING**!!

www.madamandeve.co.za

Panel 9: SHUT UP, YOU CAPTURED RADICAL ECONOMIC TRANSFORMATION SPIN DOCTOR!

OH, YEAH?!

WHATEVER HAPPENED TO OLD-FASHIONED NAME CALLING?

©RAPID PHASE. 2017

Panel 10: YO MAMA!

AH. THAT'S MORE LIKE IT.

Panel 11: YO MAMA IS A **WHITE MONOPOLY CAPITAL STOOGE**!

≥SIGH.≤

www.madamandeve.co.za

MADAM & Eve
BY STEPHEN FRANCIS & RICO

A FAMOUS YOUNG WIZARD.

...WITH THE POWER OF RADICAL ECONOMIC TRANSFORMATION.

...PREPARES TO DO BATTLE WITH DARK COUNTER-REVOLUTIONARY FORCES.

TO SAVE HIS FRIENDS, IT'S A FIGHT HE CANNOT AFFORD TO LOSE...

ULTIMATELY, HE WILL HAVE TO FACE AND CAPTURE HIS BIGGEST FOE!

Harry Bell Pottinger
AND THE
PRISONER *of* WHITE MONOPOLY CAPITAL

Coming soon to ANN7.